The Healing Touch of

Reiki

By

P.B.V. Lakshmi
&
P.V.S. Sastry

PUSTAK MAHAL®

The Usui System of Natural Healing

Copernicus proved
that the hands
that serve are
holier than the
lips that pray.

Where there is faith,
there is love.
Where there is love
there is peace.
Where there is peace
there is God.
Where there is God
there is no need.

DEDICATION

With Love, Gratitude & Respect to the world famous Reiki Masters: Mr. Mikao Usui, • Dr. Chujiro Hayashi • Hawayo Takata • Barbara Weber Ray • Maureen O'Toole • Kate Nani • Paula Horan • Barbara Szepan • Pravin D. Patel • Parinda Macwana.

We also express our gratitude to the readers who chose to hold this book in their hands.

Publishers
Pustak Mahal®

Administrative office and sale centre

J-3/16 , Daryaganj, New Delhi-110002
☎ 23276539, 23272783, 23272784 • *Fax:* 011-23260518
E-mail: info@pustakmah il.com • *Website:* www.pustakmahal.com

Branches
Bengaluru: ☎ 080-22234025 • *Telefax:* 080-22240209
E-mail: pustakmahalblr@gmail.com
Mumbai: ☎ 022-22010941, 022-22053387
E-mail: unicornbooksmumbai@gmail.com
Patna: ☎ 0612-3294193 • *Telefax:* 0612-2302719
E-mail: rapidexptn@gmail.com

© **Pustak Mahal, New Delhi**

ISBN 978-81-223-0701-6

Edition: 2017

Printed at : AR Emm International, Delhi

Contents

Preface

Reiki is the simplest form of healing the body, mind, and spirit. In short, it can be termed as "God's love in its purest form and is completely unconditional and demands neither of the giver nor of the receiver". In this book, the authors have made it easy to understand the definition, meaning, concept and advantages of Reiki.

This book is a complete guide for Reiki practitioners and healers. It gives knowledge about the Chakras, Endocrine system, Aura etc., whose understanding is necessary for Reiki practice to cure different diseases.

The book will serve as the complete text manual for persons learning Reiki. An attempt has been made to demystify the hidden facts about Aura and its connection with the physical body. Also an integrated and holistic approach has been adopted for various topics covered in this book such as Aura, Chakras, Endocrine system and the magic healing through mental affirmations. The authors have benefitted from regular practice of the positive affirmations as mentioned by Louis Hay. They strongly believe that through regular practice with faith one can heal oneself through mental affirmations i.e. "The mental cause of physical illness and the metaphysical ways to overcome it." In this healing, positive attitude plays an important role.

It is worthwhile to mention here that myths and pre-conceived notions that "Reiki is used only to cure diseases" are not correct. Rather, Reiki is a technique which can heal anyone in any situation.

— P.B.V. LAKSHMI
&
P.V.S. SASTRY

Rei   **ki**

Rei means "Spirit" or "Soul".

Ki means "energy" and is originally connected to a sense of air or atmosphere which pervades and surrounds the universe.

These Japanese ideograms therefore embody the concept of a universal life force appropriate to healing an all-enveloping energy of body, soul and spirit.

Acknowledgement

Perhaps one of the most rewarding experiences in writing this book on Reiki, is the meeting of like-minds and loving cooperation of many people, friends, enlightened healers and teachers and even casual acquaintances. There was something so affable in them that by the time the book was finished, we were imbued with a warm feeling of God's grace profoundly acting in this creative venture.

We thank our parents for giving us birth to bear the torch of an honest work and a generous mission to spread the message of consciousness and transparent living by the power of 'Reiki' mantra which works for a peaceful, harmonious and holistic life.

We also extend our sincere regards to all Reiki masters and teachers, from Dr. Mikao Usui to Mrs. Parinda Macwana, for having inspired us to practise the sublime science of Reiki and preach the universal message of unconditional love.

To Mrs. Parinda Macwana, we acknowledge our special gratitude who endeared us to Reiki and groomed us into Reiki masters with great love and care. Reiki practice has brought in a remarkable positive revolution in our lives.

Also, our thanks to all students and friends who helped us in sharing their views and suggestions on alternative medicines and valuable insights in Reiki.

The invaluable cooperation from Mr. K.V.S. Subrahmanyam and Mrs K. Janaki, in conducting many seminars and workshops in India, needless to say, calls for a very special appreciation and thanks. We are indebted to our children, Prashant and Arvind, for their unconditional support and for entering the full data in the computer and taking prints with much diligence.

Thanks to Ms. Pallavi Nautiyal for rendering fine drawings of the Chakras. We conclude with thanks also to few non-Reiki critics for their constructive criticism of our earlier book—**Reiki, the First Degree Manual.**

— P.B.V. LAKSHMI
&
P.V.S. SASTRY

1. The Art of Reiki

What is Holistic Medicine?

The adjective "holistic" is derived from the ancient Greek word "holos" which means "whole". Interest in the holistic approach to medicine was revived in the early 1970s. The idea of holism and the word itself were first introduced by the South African statesman and biologist Jan Christian Smuts in his book **Holism and Evolution** as early as in 1926. To Smuts, holism was a way of viewing and describing living things including people, as entities greater than and different from the sum of their parts.

Holistic medicine is also an alternative to a scientific approach that attempts to understand all phenomena including human beings by reducing them to their most basic biological processes. A good number of people who matter, feel that the focus of modern Western medicine is too impersonal and narrow; that many doctors tend to view their patients as biological machines rather than human beings.

Holistic medicine does not neglect the need for swift and sophisticated medical or surgical action, but does emphasize health promotion and patient education. It respects the capacity people have for healing themselves and regards them as active partners in health care, rather than passive recipients. Apart from relying on modern technology and medicines, whenever necessary, holistic medicine welcomes all the techniques that have been developed in other cultures and at other times. Thus, it makes use of a variety of therapeutic approaches. These approaches have sometimes been described as "Alternative" or "Complementary" Medicine (e.g. : Homoeopathy, Ayurveda, Acupuncture, etc.)

The Holistic Approach to Medicine includes:

a. Humanistic medicine, which emphasizes the relationship between physicians and patients, and the psychological and spiritual development of both the patient and physician,

b. Psychosomatic medicine, which is concerned with the interdependence and mutual influence of psychological and physical factors, and

c. Behavioural medicine, which stresses the psychological and social causes and effects of illness.

Holism has always been vital to healing, and some of history's most gifted physicians have embraced holistic beliefs. The ancient Greek physician Hippocrates, writing in the 5th century B.C. emphasized the environmental causes, the importance of emotional factors and nutrition, health and disease.

A holistic physician is someone who promotes well-being through educational means and encourages self-care. He treats illness with a holistic approach.

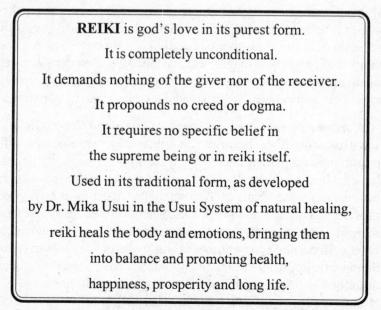

REIKI is god's love in its purest form.

It is completely unconditional.

It demands nothing of the giver nor of the receiver.

It propounds no creed or dogma.

It requires no specific belief in

the supreme being or in reiki itself.

Used in its traditional form, as developed

by Dr. Mika Usui in the Usui System of natural healing,

reiki heals the body and emotions, bringing them

into balance and promoting health,

happiness, prosperity and long life.

Ref: Dr. James S. Gordon, M.D., Dept. of Family Medicine, George Town University Medical School, Washington D.C.

Reiki

What is Reiki

The word **Reiki** means Universal Life Force Energy. It is defined as that power which acts and lives in all created matter. The word Reiki consists of two parts. The syllable **REI** describes the universal, boundless aspect of the energy while **KI** stands for the vital life force energy which flows through all living beings. It is one of the highest forms of energy in existence.

*Everyone is born with **Reiki** for it is the energy of life itself.*

What Reiki is Not

Reiki is not a religion, as it holds no creed or doctrine. It has nothing to do with spiritualism or the occult in any shape or form. It has nothing to do with the invoking of ghosts or demons, nor is it concerned with hypnosis or any other psychological technique. To practise Reiki, no special kind of faith or belief is required.

In Reiki treatment, use is made solely of natural but concentrated form of cosmic energy.

History of Reiki

Throughout the history of mankind, healing methods have always existed which were based on the transfer of universal, all pervading, life energy, the same energy which brings forth all life in the universe and nourishes it. Even thousands of years ago, the Tibetans had a deep understanding of the nature of spirit, energy and matter. They used this knowledge to heat their bodies, harmonize their souls and lead their spirit to experience of unity.

This knowledge was guarded and preserved by the mystery school of most ancient cultures and was available in its entirety only to very few people, usually priests or spiritual leaders who in turn passed it on to their disciples by word of mouth. The knowledge of **Reiki** would have remained hidden forever had not Dr. Mikao Usui rediscovered the key which led to the recovery of a thousand-year old tradition of healing in 2500-year-old Sanskrit Sutras at the end of the 19th century.

How is Reiki Learnt

The key to Reiki is its simplicity. The real difference is in the Attunement (also known as initiation) Process, which the student experiences in the various levels of Reiki classes.

During the first degree seminar (approx. 16-20 hours, spread over a period of two days), a series of four attunements are given by Traditional Reiki Master. In the process, certain energy centres, also known as Chakras, are opened to enable the person to channel (and vibrate) higher amount of Universal Life Force Energy.

After this, one can lay one's hands on the other person and help accelerate the healing process by transferring Reiki. The other person draws in just the right amount of this life force energy through the hands of a Reiki Channel that he/she needs to release, activate or transform the energy of the physical, mental and etheric bodies.

Reiki is a natural system of great simplicity, since to practise it you only need your hands and nothing else. Where other forms of therapy may demand months and years of training for the practitioner, Reiki can be taught in a weekend. After having been through the attunement process, most nurses, doctors, massage therapists, and people well acquainted with the touch and feel of the human body, notice immediate increase in the amount of energy or the feeling of heat emanating from their hands when doing treatments.

Immediate relief can be attained in all kinds of complaints. Today, we can use Reiki to complement all other healing methods.

Effects of Reiki Treatment

Once a person is attuned, he or she needs only to have a desire to do Reiki on himself/herself or others, and the energy is immediately drawn on its own accord; no further intense focus from the practitioner is needed.

Reiki is an extremely effective technique of total relaxation and stress release. One is filled with a sensation of peace, vitality and joy, often combined with a pleasant feeling of security and of being enclosed in a fine sheath of energy. Treating oneself also helps to release withheld emotions and energy blocks.

Reiki works holistically. It can not only effect changes in the chemical structure of the body by helping to regenerate organs and rebuild tissue and bones, but also help create a mental balance. Reiki is a wonderful tool to help one develop conscious awareness, the very key to enlightenment.

Reiki affects each individual in a very personal way, the result being determined by the needs of the person being treated. Some common denominators which seem to result from most treatments are given below. Reiki

- balances energy
- increases creativity
- helps release emotions
- releases stress
- amplifies energy
- works on causal level of disease
- heals holistically
- increases awareness
- reverses aging process.

Reiki can never do damage in any way, since it only flows in the quantities necessary for the recipient.

The Usui system of Reiki is not only the most simple and natural healing method, but it is also the most effective way of transferring the Universal Life Force Energy. Once a person has been opened up to become a "channel" for Reiki, concentrated life energy will flow through his hands on its own accord and he will retain this ability for the rest of his life.

As with most things in life, Reiki must be experienced to be appreciated. May your exploration of Reiki be a joyous one!

Chronology of Reiki Development

India

620 BCE	Birth of Gautama Siddhartha, Sakyamuni Buddha at Lumbini, India-Nepal border.
543 BCE	Death of Gautama Siddhartha at Kusinagara, India.
2nd to 1st Century BCE	Tantra Lotus Sutra written, other healing texts.
7 BCE	Birth of Jesus.
5 BCE	The "Three Wise Men" (3 Magi) come from the East (India) to seek the reincarnation of an Enlightened One. They take Jesus and family to Egypt and India.
27 or 30 CE to 30 or 33 CE	Jesus returns to Jerusalem for 2-3 years. The Crucifixion. Evidence that Jesus survived it.
46 or 49 CE	Jesus returns to India, 16 years after the Crucifixion.
110 CE	Death of Jesus in Srinagar, India. Legends say he lived to 120 years of age, not unusual for his time.

Japan

Late 1800's	Mikao Usui'a quest for Reiki.
1925	Chujiro Hayashi receives the Reiki Master's degree (Reiki III) at the age of 47.
1930	Death of Mikao Usui. He made 16-18 Reiki Masters, sources vary.
May 10, 1941	Death of Chujiro Hayashi. He made 13-16 Reiki Masters including the first woman, his wife Chie Hayashi and Hawayo Takata.

Hawaii

December 24, 1900	Birth of Hawayo Kawamuru (Takata).
March 19, 1917	Marries Saichi Takata.

October, 1930	Death of Saichi Takata.
1935	Takata goes to Japan for healing at Maeda Hospital in Alaska, then to Hayashi's Reiki clinic, Shina No Machi, Tokyo. She is healed in 4 months.
Spring, 1936	Takata receives Reiki I from Chujiro Hayashi.
Winter, 1938	Takata receives Reiki II from Hayashi and returns to Hawaii. She opens her first healing clinic in Kapaa.
December 11, 1980	Death of Hawayo Takata. She made 22 Reiki Masters from 1970-1980. Some sources give death date as December 12.

Reiki Master Lineage

Dr. Mikao Usui

★

Dr. Chujiro Hayashi

★

Hawayo Takata

★

Barbara Weber Ray

★

Maureen O'Toole

★

Kate Nani

★

Paula Horan

★

Barbara Szepan

★

Pravin D Patel

★

Parinda Macwana

17

Philosophy of Reiki

Reiki is not associated with any material which is visible, nor does it have a shape, nor name.

There exists on Supreme Being, the Absolute Infinite, a Dynamic Force that governs the world and universe. It is an unseen spiritual power that vibrates and all other powers fade into insignificance before it. Therefore, it is Absolute!

This power is unfathomable, immeasurable, and being a Universal Life Force, it is incomprehensible to man. Yet, every single living being is receiving its blessing daily, awake or asleep.

Different teachers and masters call it the Great Spirit; the Universal Life Force; Life Energy because when applied, it vitalizes the whole system; Ether Wave because it soothes pain and puts you into deep slumber as if under an anaesthetic; and the Cosmic Wave because it radiates vibrations of exultant feeling and lifts you into harmony.

Reiki is a radionic wave like radio. It could be applied locally or, as in short wave, a distant treatment could also be successfully given.

Reiki is neither electricity, nor radium, nor X-ray. It could penetrate thin layers of silk, linen, porcelain or lead, wood or steel, because it comes from the Great Spirit, the Infinite.

It does not destroy delicate tissues or nerves, it is absolutely harmless; therefore, it is a practical and safe treatment. Because it is a universal wave, everything that has life benefits when treated *viz.* plant life, fowls, animals as well as human beings, infant or old, poor or rich.

It should be applied and used daily as prevention. God gave us this body, a place to dwell, and our daily bread. We were put into this world for some purpose. Therefore, we should have health and happiness.

It was God's plan, so He provided us with everything. He gave us hands to use them to apply and heal, to retain physical health and mental balance, to free ourselves from ignorance and live in an enlightened world, to live in harmony with ourselves and others, and love all beings.

When these rules are applied daily, the body shall respond and all we wish and desire to attain in this world is within reach—health, happiness and the road to longevity. Being a universal force from the Great Divine Spirit, Reiki belongs to all who seek and desire to learn the art of healing.

Reiki knows neither colour, nor creed, nor age—old or young. It will find its way when the student is ready to accept it. He is shown the way. Initiation is a sacred ceremony and the contact is made. Because we are associating with the Divine Spirit, there is no error nor should we doubt. It is Absolute!

With the first contact or initiation, the hands radiate vibrations when applied to the ailing part. It relieves pain, stops the blood from an open wound; your hands are ready to heal acute and chronic diseases, in the human beings, plants, fowls, and animals. In acute cases, Reiki application for only a few minutes is necessary. In chronic cases, the first step is to find the cause and effect.

It is not necessary to undress the patient completely, but it is better to loosen all tight clothing so that the patient may relax, lying on the table face up. Most important is to find the cause of the illness.

Start treatment from 17 points on the front. Turn patient over, treat the 7 points on the back.

During the treatment, trust your hands. Listen to vibrations or reaction. If there is pain, it registers as pain in your finger tips and palm. If the patient has itch, you get itch in your hand. If the disease is deep and chronic, it gives a deep pain; if it is acute, the pain is a shallow tingle. ·

As soon as the body responds to the treatment, the acute ailment disappears but the cause remains. Dig into the cause daily and with each treatment the cause starts dissipating.

After thus treated, finish the treatment with a balancing which adjusts the aura. Place the forefinger and second finger on both sides of the spinal column and give three downward strokes to the end of spinal chord. Only in diabetic cases are the strokes reversed.

19

The above treatment is called the foundation and it requires an hour or more, all depending on the complications and seriousness of the case.

Going through the body in minute detail, the hands become sensitive and are able to determine the cause and detect the slightest congestion within, whether physical or mental, acute or chronic. Being strictly drugless and a bloodless treatment, Reiki will adjust the body to normal.

In about four days to three weeks, we find a great change taking place within the body; all internal organs and glands will begin to function with much vigour and rhythm.

The digestive juices are put out in a normal flow, the congested nerves slacken, the adhesions break away, the lazy colon gets organized, the faecal matter drops from the walls of the intestines, and the gases eliminate.

The toxin, accumulated in the body over many years, finds its way out through the pores. It is a sticky perspiration. The bowels increase, become dark and strong in odour. The urine increases like dark tea, sometimes white as if flour is stirred in water. It lasts four to six days. All the above mentioned beneficial changes result from just one treatment.

When your body has undergone these changes, you are assured of a big general overhaul of the intestinal organs taking place. With such good cleansing, the body becomes active. The numbed nerves regain sense of feeling, appetite increases, sound sleep becomes natural, eyes sparkle, and skin glows like silk. With new blood and good circulation, nerves and glands restored, it is possible to rejuvenate your body for five to ten years.

At the time of Reiki treatment, it is very important what you consume. With proper food the patient responds faster to the treatments.

In the Reiki health treatments, we are vegetarians, and eat all kinds of seasonal fruits. Nature provides with plenty, but never to waste. Overeating is a sin. Eat in moderation, with a feeling of gratitude, to recognize the Great Spirit who is the creator, who is the All Power to make things grow and blossom and bear fruit.

Come to the table with pleasant thoughts. Never eat when you are worried. Milk, white sugar, and starches are to be avoided when the patient has a weak stomach.

■ ■ ■

2. Uses of Reiki

History of the Usui System of Natural Healing

The story of Reiki to date has been an oral history that is passed on from teacher to student by the word of mouth. This is the story as I and others have heard it.

The founder of Reiki as natural healing is Dr. Mikao Usui. At the turn of the century, late 1800's, Dr. Usui was the president of a small Christian University in Kyoto, Japan Doshishua University. He was also a Christian minister.

Dr. Mikao Usui

An interaction with a student during a Sunday service, changed the focus of Dr. Usui's life. As Dr. Usui was beginning one of the last Sunday services of the school year, a senior student, about to graduate, asked Dr. Usui:

"Do you accept the contents of the Bible literally?"

Dr. Usui answered that indeed he did. The student went on to say:

"The Bible says that Jesus cured the sick, that he healed, and that he walked on water. You accept this as written, have you ever seen this happen?"

The student continued:

"For you, Dr. Usui, that kind of blind faith is enough, for you have lived your life and are secure. For us who are just beginning our adult lives and who have many questions and concerns, it is not enough. We need to see with our own eyes."

A seed had been sown. The next day, Dr. Usui resigned his position as president of Doshishua University and went to the University of Chicago in the United States where he received a doctorate degree in scripture trying to uncover the secret of how Jesus and his disciples healed the sick.

However, he could not find what he sought. Realizing that in the Buddhist tradition it is held that the Buddha had the power to heal, Dr. Usui decided to return to Japan and see what he could learn from Buddhism.

Upon his return to Japan, Dr. Usui began to visit the Buddhist monasteries searching for someone who had an interest in and some knowledge of physical healing. He always received the same answer to his inquiries:

"We are too busy with healing the spirit to worry about healing the body."

After a long search he found someone who was at least interested in the problem of physical healing, an elderly abbot of a Zen monastery.

Dr. Usui requested that he be admitted to the monastery so that he could study the Buddhist scriptures, the sutras, in search of the key of healing. He was admitted and so began his study.

He studied the Japanese translations of the Buddhist scriptures but did not find the explanation he sought. He learned Chinese so that a wider range of Buddhist writings were available to him. But, still he could not succeed in his mission.

Dr Usui then decided to learn Sanskrit, the ancient language, so that he could read the original Buddhist writings and have access to those writings that had never been translated into another language.

Finally, he found what he had been looking for. In the teachings of the Buddha that had been written down by some unknown disciple as the Buddha spoke, Dr. Usui found the formula, the symbols, the description of how Buddha healed.

So, at the end of a seven-year search, although Dr. Usui had uncovered the knowledge, he did not have the power to heal. Discussing this with his old friend, the abbot, he decided to go to a mountain and meditate, to seek the power to heal. The abbot told him that it could be dangerous, that he could lose his life. Dr. Usui answered that he had come this far and would not turn back.

Dr. Usui climbed one of the sacred mountains of Japan and meditated for twenty-one days. On the first day, he placed twenty-one small stones in front of him, and as each day passed he threw one away.

On the 21st day, Dr. Usui became aware of a beam of light from the heavens that came shooting towards him. Although he was afraid, he did not move but was struck by the light and knocked over. Then in a rapid succession he saw before him bubbles of light, the symbols that he had discovered in his study, the key to the healing by Buddha and Jesus. The symbols burned themselves into his memory.

When the trance was over, Dr. Usui no longer felt exhausted, stiff, or hungry as he had felt moments before on that last day of his meditation. He got up and began to walk down the mountain. On his way he stubbed his big toe, tearing back the toenail. He jumped with pain and grabbed his toe with his hand. In minutes the pain left, the bleeding stopped and his toe was well on the way to healing.

When Dr. Usui got off the mountain, he stopped at an outside vendor's stall and ordered breakfast. The old man at the stall, seeing the length of his facial hair and the condition of his clothes, realized that he had been on a long fast and said that it would be a few minutes before he could prepare his food so that it would not upset his long empty stomach. He directed Dr. Usui to go and sit under a tree on a bench and wait.

Soon the granddaughter of the old man came with his breakfast. As he looked at her, Dr. Usui saw that she had been crying and that her face was swollen and red on one side.

He asked her what was wrong and she replied that she had a toothache for three days. He asked if he could touch her face, and with her permission he cupped her cheeks in his hands. In a few minutes the pain left her and the swelling began to recede.

Returning to the monastery in the evening, Dr. Usui was told that his friend, the abbot, was in bed, suffering from a painful attack of arthritis. After bathing and having something to eat, Dr. Usui went to see his friend and with his healing hands, relieved his pain.

For the next seven years, Dr. Usui worked in a beggar camp in Japan, healing the sick. Those that were young and able, he sent off to find work. After seven years, he began to see those inmates of the beggar camp he had helped heal, were returning back in the same condition that he had found them.

He asked them why they had returned to the camp. They answered that they preferred their old way of life. Dr. Usui realized that he had healed sickness of the physical body but had not taught appreciation for life or a new way of living. He left the beggar camp and began to teach others who wished to know more. He taught them how to heal themselves and gave them the Principles of Reiki to help heal their thoughts.

One of these students, Churio Hayashi, a retired Naval Officer, was seeking a way to serve others. Dr. Usui initiated him in the Reiki practice and he became deeply involved in this healing method.

When Usui's life was drawing to a close, he recognized Dr. Hayashi as the master of Reiki and gave him the responsibility of keeping the essence of his teachings intact.

Dr. Hayashi, realizing the importance of a system and record keeping, founded a clinic in Tokyo where people could come for treatment and to learn Reiki. The clinic also had practitioners who would go out to treat those who could not come to the clinic.

Dr. Hayashi left records demonstrating that Reiki finds the source of the physical symptoms of the disease, fills the vibration or energy need, and restores the body to wholeness.

One day in 1935, a young woman from Hawaii was brought to the clinic by an employee of a surgical hospital in Tokyo. This woman, Hawayo Takata, had come to Japan to have an operation for a tumour. As Mrs. Takata prepared herself for the surgery, she had a sense that the operation was not necessary and that there was another way of treatment. She had been led to Reiki.

Following Mrs. Takata's experiences and treatments at the clinic, her illness lessened and her desire to learn Reiki grew. When her treatments were almost finished, she requested to be admitted to a beginning class. But, she was not given admission. She realized that she must demonstrate a deep commitment to Reiki. She went to Dr. Hayashi and told him of her feelings and her willingness to stay in Japan as long as was necessary. He consented to begin her training.

Mrs. Takata, with her two daughters, stayed in Japan with the Hayashi family for a year, learning Reiki through daily practice under Hayashi's guidance. When both felt the training was complete, Mrs. Takata returned to Hawai with her gift of healing,

In Hawaii, Mrs. Takata's practice flourished and soon Dr. Hayashi and his daughter came to visit her. They stayed several months teaching, training, and being with Mrs. Takata. In February, 1938, Mrs. Takata was initiated as a Master of the Usui System of

26

natural healing. Soon after the initiation, Hayashi and his daughter returned to Japan.

Dr. Hayashi had sensed that a war was imminent between the United States and Japan. He could not reconcile being a Reiki Master and having to serve again in the Navy. He began to set the affairs of his household in order.

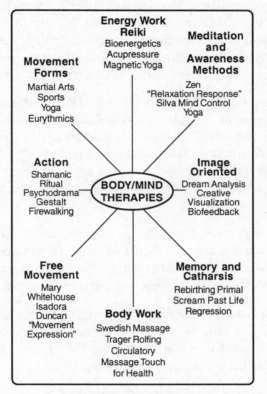

Body/Mind Therapies

During this time, Mrs. Takata in Hawaii had a vivid dream that caused her concern. She knew she must go to Japan and be with Dr. Hayashi. When she arrived, Dr. Hayashi told her many things: that the war was coming; who would win; what she must do and where she must go to avoid trouble for herself as she was a Japanese-American living in Hawaii. All these things he foresaw and passed on to her for her protection and for the protection of Reiki.

When all of his business was taken care of and in order, Dr. Hayashi called his family together along with the Reiki Masters. Giving them his final words and recognizing Mrs. Takata as his successor in Reiki, he said good-bye. Sitting in the formal Japanese manner and dressed in his formal Japanese clothing, he closed his eyes and left his body.

Following his guidance, Mrs. Takata finished her work in Japan and sailed to Hawaii. She returned as the Master of Reiki. She demonstrated her commitment throughout her life, teaching and practising Reiki. She became a powerful healer and a great teacher, introducing the gift of Reiki to the Western world.

As a young child, Phyllis Furumoto received the first degree initiation from her grandmother, Mrs. Hawayo Takata, and would treat the latter when she visited. Phyllis' life was directed into college and then a career. Although Mrs. Takata asked periodically if she would take up the study of Reiki, Phyllis felt too busy. Then in the late seventies, when Phyllis was 27, she accepted the second degree initiation.

Mrs. Takata began training Phyllis in the spring of 1976, after a month of consideration. Phyllis decided to travel and work with her grandmother. Just before the first trip, Mrs. Takata initiated Phyllis as a Master. Thereafter, her teaching and training began in earnest.

During the classes in the following year, Phyllis learned that she was to succeed Mrs. Takata Sensei in the Reiki lineage. Shortly after this acknowledgement of Phyllis as the Master of Reiki, Mrs. Takata made her transition in December, 1980.

In the years since Mrs. Takata's passing, Phyllis has accepted her role and understood the responsibility of her position. She exemplifies what does happen when one accepts the energy force of Reiki as a teacher and guide in life.

Today the Usui System of Natural Healing is practised all over the world. You are a part of this history. With your willingness to share this gift, you support and quicken the unfolding of life.

Reiki Healers

(Adapted from Reader's Digest Guide
to Alternative Medicines)

The Reiki healers use prayer, meditation, or visualization to link themselves to divine or mystical healing forces which are then channelised to patients, activating their power to heal themselves. The patients may not even know that they are being healed, although most healers will send healing only when requested by a patient. Healers usually discover this ability by accident, and see it as a gift, which they must use in the service of others. Most regard themselves as channels for powers which come from beyond them, and not as being personally able to heal. Often training or religious belief helps them to develop their gifts. Many such healers belong to church or spiritual groups. They work as one or in groups, and regular meetings are held at which people are prayed for or meditated upon.

Any mental, physical or spiritual distress can be treated. The patient taking no active part, may still benefit, although it is thought that a relaxed, positive patient may be more receptive to healing energies liberated within him. Because the patient does not have to participate actively, Reiki is said to be particularly suitable for babies, young children and animals, for very ill or unconscious patients, or for the mentally challenged. Chronically ill people, whose vitality and self-healing powers have been exhausted by lengthy illness, may gain special benefit. Reiki is also particularly suitable for those who are too ill to travel.

Most healers offer their services for a small fee. Healers will not promise results or claim cures in accordance with the normal ethical approach to their art & practice which is expected by those they try to help. Other healers, who do make claims for themselves, may not necessarily be charlatans, their claims may simply reflect an absolute faith in the power they work with. Healers do not attempt to examine or diagnose patients, and will advise you to see a doctor if you have not already done so.

Helping patients to heal themselves is usually a gradual process. Instant cures cannot be expected, especially where illness is the result of long-term factors such as unhealthy diet or ongoing stress. In such cases, healing may help, but it is not offered as a replacement for more direct, orthodox therapies. Often healing is sought as a last resort when the body's defences are already depleted. Although it has proved successful in some cases regarded by orthodox medicine as incurable, patients should not expect healing to succeed immediately where all else has failed. Progress is very often slow, sometimes even preceded by worsening symptoms as the body seeks to regain its ability to fight the illness. Healers never accept that a case may be incurable, and this alone encourages many seriously ill patients. Healing of any type is likely to produce positive psychological effects. Even in cases where a condition cannot be reversed or improved, a patient may be relieved of distress and brought to accept his or her condition. Many people even experience a sense of inner harmony through this kind of therapy. The only danger arises when conventional treatment, which may help, is neglected in favour of Reiki, which may not. Reiki can do

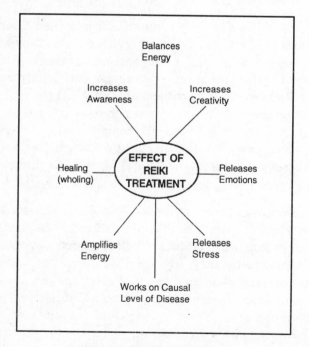

Effect of Reiki Treatment

no harm, provided it does not take the place of other treatment and the patient's hopes are not raised unrealistically.

Chakras

We understand our physical framework, i.e. our body, as an energy body but not just muscle and bone. Situated with the body is a complex network through which the energy flows. This network consists of channels called nerves, which distribute vital energy to each and every part of the body.

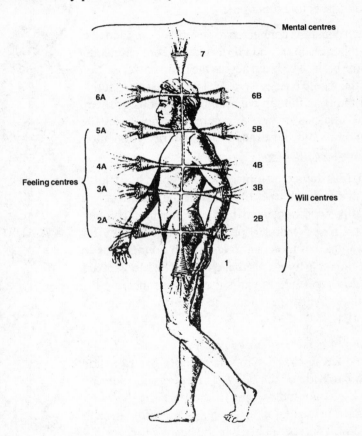

Fig 1A: *Location of the Seven Major Chakras*

Within this network, there are some major centres called energy centres or chakras which help in the distribution of energy. For example, the solar plexus is the energy centre which is called

'Manipura Chakra'. This chakra helps in distributing energy to the organs around the area of its influence, i.e. liver, pancreas, stomach etc. Hence Manipura chakra helps in burning of food. Kidneys and the adrenal gland are also associated with this chakra. If this centre is unable to distribute energy properly, the person may show malfunction of the digestive system, i.e. indigestion. In fact, all the chakras are connected to particular organs and responsible for their respective functions.

Each chakra is connected to several organs and also to other chakras, and all the chakras are connected to the brain. The brain acts as the main power-station of the whole energy system. The chakras are active all the time though we are not conscious of them. The chakras draw the cosmic energy from the universe and the organs draw energy from their respective chakras.

Chakras depict the lotus. Each chakra is like a lotus with a fixed number of petals. If the chakra is in a healthy condition, it will be like a lotus in full bloom. The Crown chakra is opened towards the sky for the intake of the cosmic energy. It connects us to the universe by a 'spiritual chord'. The Mooladhara chakra is opened towards the earth connecting the body to the earth. It acts like an earthing. (Fig. 1A & 1B)

The chakras exist on each layer of our 'AURA' also. These chakras appear on both the frontside and backside of the body. The energy is taken by each chakra and is sent to the parts of the body located in the major nerve plexus area close to each chakra. This energy helps in the healthy functioning of the 'Auric' field and the physical body. This energy is called 'PRANA'. If a chakra stops functioning properly, it will not be able to take energy properly. This means that the body organs served by that chakra will not get the required energy. If

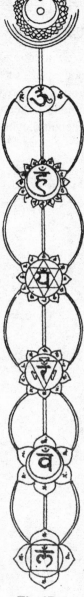

Fig. 1B:
Sounds of the Chakras

this continues, normal functioning of the organs and other body parts attached to that chakra will be disrupted. Hence, that part of the body will weaken and become diseased.

Several Upanishads have depicted the number of chakras as 212, 189, 144, 108, 24 and 7 (in fact only six major chakras). There are five types of chakras, namely Major, Minor, Macro, Mini and Micro. The significance of the number mentioned above can be explained as follows: The reason why the 'Gayatri Mantra' (hailed as the 'Maha Mantra') is so popular, is that it contains 24 bijaksharas, which on chanting will activate the major and minor chakras. The reason why people of all religions chant a hymn or a mantra with the help of a chain of 108 beads is to activate all the five types of chakras that exist in a human body both at the physical and Auric levels. I would like to concentrate only on the seven major chakras.

Each chakra is like a funnel both to the frontside and backside of the body. Each funnel has its water opening on the outside of our body about six inches in diameter, one inch from the body. The other end of the chakras is like a tip attached to the spine.

The first major chakra, 'Mooladhara' (Fig. 2), is located at the tip of the spinal cord opening towards the earth. It is related to our

Fig. 2: *Mooladhara Chakra*

33

will to live and supplies the body with physical vitality. It supplies energy to the spinal cord, the adrenal gland, and the kidneys.

The second chakra, 'Swadhisthana' (Fig. 3), is located just above the pubic bone on the front and back side of the body. This chakra helps us to sense emotions. It is related to our sensuality and sexuality. It supplies energy to our sex organs and immune system.

Fig. 3: *Swadhisthana Chakra*

The third chakra, 'Manipura' (Fig. 4), is located in the solar plexus area on the front and back side of the body (at the junction between the last thoracic vertebra and the first lumber vertebra). It supplies energy to the organs in this area like stomach, spleen, liver, gall bladder and pancreas.

The fourth chakra, 'Anahata' (Fig. 5), is located in the heart area. It supplies energy to our heart, circulatory system, thymus and upper back. It is the chakra which is related to love and will. It is this centre through which we express our unconditional love to fellow beings. It is a very important chakra in the healing process. All energy that we get and send to others goes through heart chakra into our hands.

34

Fig. 4: *Manipura Chakra*

Fig. 5: *Anahata Chakra*

35

The fifth chakra, 'Vishuddha' (Fig. 6), is located in the front and backside of the throat, supplying energy to the thyroid, bronchi, lungs and the elementary canal. If this chakra is opened, one is successful in his communication skills which help a person in his daily life and work-place.

Fig. 6: *Vishuddha Chakra*

The sixth chakra, 'Ajna' (Fig. 7), is located on the forehead and back of the head, supplying energy to the pituitary gland, lower brain, left eye, ears, nose etc. It is associated with the capacity to visualize and also develop intuition and clairvoyance.

The seventh chakra, 'Sahasra' (Fig. 8), is directly related to the spirituality, a state which is beyond the physical world. It is the state of experience of directly knowing one's own inner self. It supplies energy to the upper brain, right eye, etc. We are connected to the universe with the help of this chakra through a spiritual chord.

It is important to open the chakras and increase our energy flow because the more energy we let flow, the healthier we are. The imbalance in the energy causes illness. Our sense organs and the senses are also associated with our chakras.

Fig. 7: *Ajna Chakra*

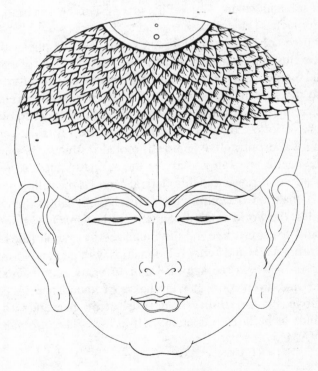

Fig. 8: *Sahasra Chakra*

37

The detailed information about each major chakra is given below:

1. **Mooladhara :** Mooladhara means foundation. It is the lowest of the chakras. It is known as the root centre because it is the seat of dwelling place of primal energy. Mooladhara is like a lotus with four petals. It is also the seat of Kundalini shakti. Normally, the Kundalini is in the form of a serpent in deep sleep, coiled around the 'Swayambhu linga'. It is the source of all energy, may it be mental, emotional, spiritual or sexual. The energy is only one but the centre, through which it manifests, gives it various qualities and attributes. This energy can be awakened or activated through concentrating the mind, exercises and self-purification. The energy achieved can lead to Sahasra, where this pure energy unites with pure consciousness. The *bija mantra* is **'LAM'**.

2. **Swadhisthana :** Swadhisthana means one's own abode ('swa' — self and 'sthan' — dwelling place). This chakra is above the Mooladhara chakra in the spinal region. It is symbolized by an orange coloured lotus with six petals. On the physical level, Swadhisthana is mainly associated with the organs of excretion and reproduction. Vitalisation of this centre can therefore rectify any disorder in these functions. On a deeper level, this chakra is the seat of the unconscious mind, the collective consciousness. It has a lot of collected ancestral memories. It is the centre of man's most primitive and deep-rooted instincts. By purifying this centre one can rise above the animal nature. A person's creativity is present in this chakra. Moon is the ruling planet of this chakra. Concentrating on this chakra enables the mind to reflect the world as the moon reflects the sun. One acquires the ability to use creative and sustaining energy to sublimate himself to refined arts and better relationships with others. Normally, a person between the age of 8 and 14 years acts from second chakra's motivation. It is a chakra of abundance. A person, whose *swadhisthana* is active, often pretends to be a prince or hero. He maintains self-esteem. The *bija mantra* is **'WAM'**.

3. **Manipura :** Manipura means the 'city of jewels' ('Mani'—gem, 'pura' — city). As the name indicates, this chakra is the fire centre, the focal point of heat, and is lustrous like a jewel, radiant with vitality and energy. It is like a bright yellow-coloured lotus with ten petals. The organs attached to this chakra are the organs of digestion like liver, pancreas, gall bladder, stomach etc. and also the glands present on the kidneys. The production & secretion of enzymes is very important for the proper digestion and absorption of food materials. Manipura chakra is the subtle centre, which controls these activities. Adrenalin is an emergency hormone secreted by adrenal gland and its secretion is controlled by Manipura chakra. Adrenalin is secreted into the blood during emergency situations and has an effect of speeding up all the physiological processes, making the mind sharp and alert. It has a direct impact in increasing the heart beat, sugar levels, and the respiration rate. Those people who suffer from laziness, sluggishness and depression or malfunctioning of digestive system, such as indigestion, etc. should concentrate on Manipura chakra. The *bija mantra* is **'RAM'.**

In some schools, like the Zen Buddhism, Manipura chakra is the most important centre and is said to be the seat of Kundalini. This is true in the sense that Kundalini goes through a transformation by passing through Manipura and is revealed more in its true light. The Kundalini, that rises from Mooladhara, splits in the Swadhisthana and flows on either side of the spinal cord. Manipura chakra is the centre of vitality in the psychic and physical bodies. The upward moving vitality i.e. 'prana' and the downward moving vitality i.e. 'aprana' meet here and heat is produced which is necessary to support life. That is the reason, the ruling element of Manipura is fire which is represented by bright yellow lotus. It is the centre of all emotions, both negative and positive. A person, whose Manipura is stimulated or activated, is free from negative emotions like jealousy, anger, fear, worry, hurry, hatred, intolerance. Between the age of 14 and 21 years, a person is ruled by Manipura chakra. Meditation on this chakra makes one realize one's errors. The balance of Manipura gives one selfless service, i.e. serving without desire for the reward.

4. **Anahata :** Anahata means unstruck ('an' — not, 'ahata' — struck). The physical organs associated with this chakra are heart and lungs, the circulatory and respiratory systems. Persons with weak Anahata chakra are sufferers of diseases like anaemia, hypertension, palpitations, tuberculosis, asthma and bronchitis. This is the chakra of love and compassion. The person with weak Anahata is unable to show his love towards the fellow beings. He is equally unable to accept love from others.

By concentrating and energizing this chakra, one masters language, poetry, his sense organs, desires etc. He gains a lot of wisdom and inner strength and it also brings about a balance of action and joy. At the age of 21-28 years, a person is governed by Anahata chakra. Concentrating on this chakra makes one aware of his karma, his life activities etc. The *bija mantra* is **'YAM'**.

5. **Vishuddha :** Vishuddha means to purify. Vishuddha chakra is located near the throat. It is the centre of purification. It is symbolized by a light blue coloured lotus with 16 petals. This chakra influences the vocal cords and the region of the larynx, thyroid & parathyroid glands. It governs the person's communication, clairvoyance. Spoken words come from this chakra, giving voice to the emotions within the heart. In this chakra all the elements of the lower chakras i.e. earth, water, fire and air are refined to their purest essence and dissolved into *akasha* (ether). Persons with weak Vishuddha chakra will have difficulty in expressing their ideas and may suffer from throat problems, hyperthyroidism, speech problems etc. Memory, ready wit, intuition are all related to this chakra. By meditating on this chakra, a person can get calmness, serenity, purity, command of speech and mantras etc.

The earth, the element of Mooladhara chakra, dissolves into water and remains in the second chakra as the essence of smell. Water of Swadhisthan chakra evaporates in the fiery Manipura chakra and remains as the essence of taste. The form of fire enters Anahata chakra and remains there as the essence of form and of vision. The air of Anahata chakra enters into Vishuddha chakra as *akasha* (ether) and becomes pure sound.

Akasha embodies the essence of all the five elements. It is without colour, smell, taste, touch, or form, free of any gross elements. The *bija mantra* is **'HAM'**.

6. **Ajna:** 'Ajna' means command or authority. This chakra is known as the third eye or Gyana chakra (eye of wisdom) or Bhrumadhya (eyebrow centre). It is also considered as Guru chakra, because through it the disciple in deeper states of meditation receives commands and guidance from his guru. This is also the chakra where one receives commands from the divine, higher self.

   Ajna chakra is symbolized as a deep blue lotus with two petals. Ajna chakra is associated with the physical organs like pineal body, a tiny pea-sized gland within the beam, which has almost atrophied in the adult human being. On the psychic planet, this point is the bridge between physical, mental and psychic bodies. By concentrating on this chakra, a person can see his future in the psychic plane. He may increase his concentration with power, memory, intelligence as these are all the powers of brain and Ajna chakra is associated with the brain. By awakening of this chakra, a person can also develop supernatural powers & supermental capabilities like clairvoyance, telepathy, intuition and other abilities which are hidden potential of every person. Thought energy also has form. When the mind is elevated and made sensitive, it is possible to send this energy through Ajna chakra. The *bija mantra* is **'AUM'**.

7. **Sahasra :** Sahasra means thousand petalled. The highest chakra, Sahasra, is the abode of pure consciousness. Through this chakra, our physical body is connected to the cosmos. It is in connection with our universe. It is symbolized by a violet lotus of thousand petals with all the alphabets of Sanskrit on them. When Kundalini awakens, it ascends through all these charas to Sahasra and merges into space from where it came. The person who meditates on Sahasra, becomes highly spiritual. He is above a normal human being and is the happiest person for he lives in thought-free, breath-free, desireless state and also leads a life without any expectations. Also the earthly pleasures and physical faculties do not bother him. He at this stage can be called as *Satchitananda* (Sat-Chit-Ananda).

Nadis: The chakras are connected to different physical organs. The energy from the chakras flows into these organs through the *nadis*. *Nadi* means flow of current. Like chakras, they are not located in the physical body. Nadis are the subtle channels through which the vital energy travels or flows. There are nearly 72,000 nadis in the body, of which 14 are important and three are the most important namely, ***Ida, Pingala and Sushumna*** (Fig. 9 & 10). Sushumna runs Mooladhara chakra, it goes to Ajna chakra. Originating from the left side of Mooladhara is the Ida nadi which goes through all the chakras and ends on the left side of Ajna chakra. From the right side of Mooladhara starts Pingala nadi which again goes through all the chakras and ends on the right side of Ajna chakra. Ida is considered as negative while Pingala is considered positive.

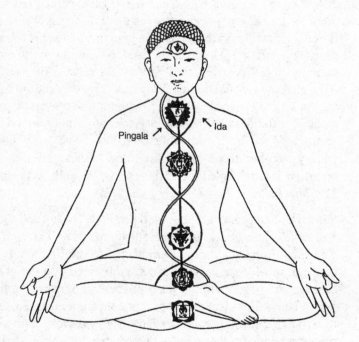

Fig. 9: *Ida and Pingala Nadis*

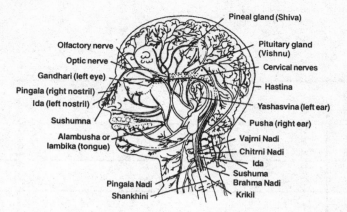

Fig. 10: *Major Nadis in the Head*

Ida and Pingala govern the opposite qualities, like Ida is mental & cold whereas Pingala is physical & hot. Every person is controlled by either Ida or Pingala at a time depending on which nadi is predominant for him at that time. This a person can make out by observing one's own breath. Normally, human beings have more flow of air through one of the nostrils only. If there is more flow of air through left nostril, Ida nadi is predominant; if there is more flow of air through right nostril Pingala nadi is predominant.

In recent times, the word nadi is translated into a nerve. So the physical nerves correspond to the physical manifestations. Two main nadis i.e. Ida & Pingala correspond to two parts of the autonomous nervous system—sympathetic and parasympathetic nervous system. Pingala coincides with the sympathetic nervous system which when activated helps the body to face emergency by increasing the heart beat, sugar level etc. Hence, if Pingala nadi is more active in a person, he will be a restless person. Ida nadi coincides with parasympathetic nervous system, which when activated, brings back the body to normalcy after it is activated. The person, whose Ida is active, is a calm person, but thinks too much. The flow of energy through Ida or Pingala is involuntary. Only by practice it can be brought under control. *Sadhakas* practise Pranayama to turn this involuntary flow of energy into voluntary one and fulfil the ultimate aim of attaining a desireless state by slowly ceasing the level of expectations.

43

Seven Chakras and their Functions

Sl. No.	Chakra	No. of Petals or Vortices	Endocrine System	Area of the Body Governed	Function	Colour	Planet	Swar	Element	Bija Mantra
1.	Sahasra	1000	Pineal gland	Upper brain and Right eye	Connects us with our Spiritual self	Violet	Sun	Ne	Ether	Ohm ॐ
2.	Ajna	2	Pituitary gland	Lower brain, left eye autonomous nervous system, hypothalamus	Intuitive centre, seat of will and clairvoyance	Indigo	Moon	Da	Ether	Aum ॐ
3.	Vishuddha	16	Thyroid	Throat, lungs	Communication, self-expression	Light blue	Mars	Pa	Ether	Gam गं
4.	Anahata	12	Thymus	Heart, blood, circulatory system, liver	Love, compassion	Green	Mercury	Ma	Air	Ham हं
5.	Manipura	10	Pancreas & Adrenals	Stomach, liver, gall bladder, nervous system	Power and wisdom centre	Yellow	Jupiter	Ga	Fire	Ram रं
6.	Svadhisthana	6	Gonads	Reproductive system	Centre of sexual energy, feeling/ emotional centre	Orange	Venus	Re	Water	Wam वं
7.	Mooladhara	4	Suprarenal	Kindneys, bladder, spine	Survival instinct, physical vitality, seat of kundalini, creative expression	Red	Saturn	Sa	Earth	Lam लं

Centring

Reiki attunements help in opening up of Chakras. Continuous Reiki treatment helps in improving intuition. If we focus our consciousness on *hara* or *chi* centre, which the Chinese call the emotional chakra, the opposite polarity chakra located in the third eye becomes balanced. When we bring the centre of our attention (i.e. the focus of our conscious awareness) into the belly chakra, we begin to connect with our true feelings. The centring meditation helps us to be centred in *hara*, and we open up to the intuitive faculties located in the third eye chakra.

The process involved is quite simple: Sit in a comfortable position on the floor with legs folded and keep your back and neck straight. Start taking long and deep breaths. Observe your breathing process. Visualize a golden ball floating above your Crown chakra. This golden ball is your conscious awareness. Continue to take long deep breaths. Inhale deeply and while exhaling, begin to see the golden ball float down through the top of your head into the Crown chakra. Visualize this golden ball merging with the violet colour spreading throughout your head region. Crown chakra is helpful in spiritual uplift. Feel that your spiritual Crown chakra is opening up, as it connects you to the universe.

Continue to take long and deep breaths. While exhaling, visualize the Golden ball separating from the violet colour of the Crown chakra and float slowly down to the Ajna chakra. Visualize the golden colour mixing with the indigo colour of the Ajna Chakra and this mixed colour spreading throughout that region. Ajna chakra helps to improve your intuition, clairvoyance. Feel that your intuitive powers, telepathy, power of clairvoyance are increasing. Continue to take long deep breaths.

Take a long, deep breath. While exhaling, visualize the golden ball separating from the Ajna chakra and floating down to the throat chakra. Vishuddha chakra's colour is light blue. Visualize the golden colour mixing with the blue colour and this mixed colour spreading throughout the throat region. This chakra helps us in communication. Feel that your communicative power is increasing. Continue to take long, deep breaths.

Take a long, deep breath. While exhaling, visualize the golden ball, separating from Vishuddha chakra and floating down to Anahata chakra. Anahata chakra is green in colour. Visualize the golden colour mixing with the green colour and spreading throughout your chest region filling your heart with the consciousness of your love. Continue breathing, as you inhale, feel the breath fill your heart with the light and energy of love, and radiating the energy of your love to all those around you. Continue to breathe slowly.

Take a long, deep breath. While exhaling, visualize the golden ball separating from Anahata chakra and floating down to the solar plexus. Visualize this golden colour mixing with the bright yellow colour of Manipura chakra and spreading throughout your solar plexus region. Feel the light and the warmth of your own power and wisdom. Manipura chakra contains all the negative emotions like anger, jealousy, fear etc. Visualize all these negative emotions burning in this yellow coloured fire. Visualize filling your chakra with positive emotions. Continue to take long, deep breaths.

Take a long, deep breath. As you exhale, visualize the golden ball separating from your Manipura chakra and floating down to the Swadhisthana chakra. Visualize this golden colour mixing with the orange colour of this chakra and spreading throughout your belly region. This is creative chakra. Feel that your creativity is increasing. Keep on breathing to your belly. Feel the peace and tranquillity. Continue to take deep, long breaths.

Take one more long breath. As you exhale, visualize the golden ball separating from Swadhisthana chakra and floating down to the Root chakra or Kundalini. Visualize the golden colour mixing with the red colour of the Root chakra and this mixed colour spreading throughout your pelvic region. Feel that your pelvic region is filling you with an overflowing abundance. Keep breathing. With every breath, feel the energy of prosperity and abundance fill your entire body.

Take a long, deep breath. As you exhale, feel the golden ball separating from your Root chakra and gently floating upwards and going back to your Hara or Swadhisthana. Continue to take long, deep breaths. As you inhale, feel the orange yellow light fill your entire body. Feel more fully grounded at the centre. Feel tranquil and totally at peace. This is the place for your higher consciousness to be centred. As you relax in this calmness, slowly begin to open your eyes and again become aware of your environment.

This meditation or exercise is designed to help you develop the feeling of being centred. As you move through each chakra, you may feel resistance at specific chakras, to the movement of your consciousness between them. If you feel blocked, you can exhale several times to remove those blockages.

Endocrine System

The human body is like a machine, which is controlled by two major systems: the nervous system and the endocrine system. The nervous system helps us to adjust to the external environment with the help of sense organs. The endocrine system (Fig. 11) brings about changes in the metabolic activities of all the body tissues. These two systems are diverse in their functions, but coordinate their activities so that the internal body harmony and balance is maintained. The *Hypothalamus,* a major nerve centre in the brain, provides the link between the brain and the endocrine system.

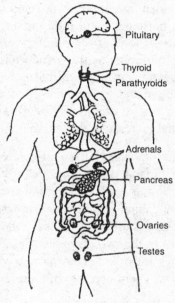

Fig. 11: *Endocrine System*

The endocrine glands present in our body make up the endocrine system. The endocrine glands are ductless glands which secrete their hormones into the extra cellular space around the cells. Thereafter, hormones are passed into the capillaries, and then further transported by the blood. These glands do not work independently. Each has a marked influence on the other.

The hormones secreted by the endocrine glands and tissues are in small quantities. The amount of hormone released is determined by the body's needs. The insufficient quantity (hyposecretion) or excess production (hypersecretion) of hormone, both cause abnormalities in the body. The hormones are specific in their action. The response, brought about in an organism by a particular hormone, cannot be induced by another hormone. Usually, hormones produced in one species show similar influence in other species. The detailed description of the important glands is as follows:

1. Pituitary Gland: It lies in the brain attached to the *Hypothalamus* by a stalk like structure. Structurally and functionally, it is divided into anterior lobe and posterior lobe. Both the lobes secrete hormones. But the most important hormone secreted by the anterior lobe of the pituitary gland is growth hormone. This growth hormone, as the name indicates, helps in growth. If the gland secretes insufficient hormone, it leads to dwarfism. If it is hyperactive and secretes more hormone than required, it leads to another kind of abnormality called *Gigantism,* in which there is abnormal increase in the length of bones.

Another important hormone secreted by the posterior lobe of the pituitary gland is *Vasporessin*. It controls the amount of water excreted in urine. If the hormone produced is less or insufficient, the kidney tubules cannot reabsorb the water and the person suffers from frequent urination. This is a disease called diabetes insipidus. Apart from the two hormones described here, the pituitary gland produces lot of other hormones which regulate so many body activities. Therefore, it is often referred to as the 'Master Gland.'

2. Thyroid Gland: The thyroid gland secretes thyroxin hormone. It is an iodine containing hormone which exerts a marked effect on the central nervous system, growth and development. The hormone regulates organic metabolism and helps in energy balance. All protein, fat and carbohydrate metabolism is influenced by thyroxin. Since the overall effect is to increase metabolism, they increase the Basal Metabolic Rate (BMR). The energy produced raises the body temperature. It also affects growth and development and increases the reactivity of the nervous system. Mineral metabolism takes place with the help of parathyroid gland present on the thyroid gland.

Excess release of thyroxin hormone accelerates the body activity, speeding up the heart and making the brain restless. It causes diseases like *Exopthalmic Goiter*. Less thyroxin leads to apathy and weight gain. It causes diseases like simple goiter. If it is produced in less quantities in children, it causes *Cretinism*. As iodine is necessary for the formation of thyroxin, it can be added to the common salt to prevent its deficiency. This is necessary in the hilly regions where soil contains very less or no iodine.

3. Adrenal Gland: The body consists of two adrenal glands, each located superior to each kidney fitting like a cap. It is also called 'Supra renal gland'. Each adrenal gland is structurally and functionally differentiated into two regions: the outer adrenal cortex and the inner adrenal medulla. Each region produces different hormones.

The most important hormone secreted by adrenal medulla is *adrenaline* or *epinephrine*. The function of adrenaline is to influence carbohydrate metabolism, increase contractibility of skeletal muscles, help the body to adapt to various extreme influences like overcooling, fasting, trauma, etc. This hormone is called emergency hormone as it prepares the body to face the emergency situations like public speaking. The final dash to win a race is under the influence of adrenaline. This helps in situations like fight or flight.

The adrenal cortex secretes many hormones, the best known is *cortisone*. In general, the cortical hormone influences carbohydrate, fat and protein metabolism and regulates salt and water balance in the body, adapts the body to stresses in extreme heat or cold, burns, inflammation.etc. Certain cortical hormones behave like sex hormones. They are both male and female hormones and occur in both the sexes. If there is an overweight of cortex in young children, this will lead to premature sexual maturity. If there is an overweight of adrenal cortex in a mature woman, she develops certain male characteristics such as beard and deep male voice. The condition is known as adrenal *virilism*. If the overgrowth occurs in mature men, they may develop some feminine characteristics such as enlargement of breasts.

49

4. Pancreas: It secretes digestive juices which help in digesting food. It also has special cells called Islets of Langerhans which secrete hormones. The cells are of different types called beta, alpha, and delta cells. The beta cells secrete insulin which is the most important hormone. It promotes glucose utilization by the body cells. It stimulates deposition of extra glucose of the blood as glycogen in liver and muscles.

Insufficient secretion of insulin causes diabetes *(Diabetes mellitus)*. Mellitus means honey, referring to the passage of sugar in urine. A diabetic person has high concentration of sugar in blood which is excreted along with urine. Oversecretion of insulin from the pancreas may show reverse effect. Sugar level in the blood is lowered and the brain may enter a state of coma if the level becomes too low. Glucose is secreted by alpha cells. It stimulates the breakdown of glycogen in the liver to glucose, thus raising the sugar level in the blood. Sometostatin secreted by gamma cells (also secreted by hypothalamus and certain intestinal cells) inhibits secretion of insulin and glucagons.

5. Gonads: Testes and ovaries. Like pancreas, the gonads are also dual in function. In addition to producing sperms and ova, they release certain important hormones called sex hormones. They show their conscious effect at the time of puberty, when secondary sexual characteristics appear. The changes, common in both sexes, include development of hair in the pubic region and in the armpits. Males have testes which produce male sex hormones and females have ovary which produce female sex hormones.

Control of hormonal secretions: The amount of hormone released by an endocrine gland is determined by the body's need for that particular hormone at any given time. The product of the target tissue exerts an effect on the respective endocrine gland. This effect may be positive (i.e. a message 'secrete more') or negative (i.e. a message 'do not secret more, slow down'). Thymus Gland behind the heart, quite big in children up to the age of 12-14 years, gets reduced in size in adults. It is supposed to be helpful in growth.

6. Pineal Gland: Pineal Gland is also an endocrine gland. The pineal gland has yet to be understood by medical scientists, for they cannot assign any definite physiological function to it. But, yoga and other holistic healers say that this gland is the link between the gross physical body and the more subtle psychic body.

7. Hypothalamus: Though hypothalamus is not part of the endocrine system, it has a great role in the body, as it controls body temperature and pituitary gland. It is present in the forebrain of the central nervous system. It is almost at the floor of the brain and includes an X-shaped optic chiasma, a hollow conical infundibulum, and a hypophysis or pituitary body. Hypothalamus is the seat of regulation of body heat.

Reiki for Control of Endocrine Glands and Hormones

We have already seen the position of seven major chakras and the associated organs in our body. If we observe, we will find that at the position of each chakra in our body, there is an endocrine gland present. As the endocrine glands maintain the coordination in the body, we can term the chakra or the endocrine gland as the energy centre of the body. Listed below are chakras and their corresponding glands.

Sahasra	:	Pituitary
Ajna	:	Hypothalamus (Though hypothalamus is not an endocrine gland, it controls the endocrine glands)
Vishuddha	:	Thyroid gland
Anahata	:	Thymus gland
Solar plexus	:	Pancreas
Swadhisthana	:	Gonads

When we give Reiki energy to a chakra, it means activating the endocrine gland at that place. With Reiki treatment, the endocrine gland receives right amount of energy and becomes balanced to produce right amount of hormone. There is neither 'hypo' nor 'hyper' secretion. If the hormones are secreted in sufficient quantity, the body maintains good and normal health. No abnormalities are there.

Aura

Very often we talk about the physical body and diseases affecting it, as we can only see our physical body. However, studies in the beginning of this century pointed to an energy field surrounding the humans and other objects. This energy field was called **Aura** by Kilner, and he observed that it differs from person to person depending on the age, sex, mental ability and health. Certain diseases showed up patches or irregularities in the Aura, which led Kilner to develop a system of diagnosis on the basis of colour, texture, volume and general appearance of Aura. Some diseases, he diagnosed in this way, were liver infection, tumours, appendicitis, epilepsy etc.

Some years ago, a group of Soviet scientists discovered that living organisms emit energy vibrations at a frequency between 300 and 2000 manometers. They called this energy the **biofield** or **bioplasma.** They found that persons capable of successful bioenergy transfer have a much wider and stronger biofield. These findings have been confirmed by the Medical Sciences Academy in Moscow and are supported by research in Great Britain, the Netherlands, Germany and Poland.

Medical experts measure electrical currents from the heart with the help of electrocardiogram (ECG) , and electrical currents from brain are measured with the help of electroencephalogram (EEG). Lie detectors measure the electropotential of the skin. They can now even measure electromagnetic fields around the body with a sensitive device called SQUID (Super Conducting Quantum Interference Device). This device does not even touch the body when measuring the magnetic field around it. SQUID is used in the USA to know the state of brain functioning. It gives more information than normal EEG.

Before the invention of SQUID, many scientists tried to invent devices to know more about the human energy field, but the first scientific evidence regarding existence of the Aura originated in

Russia. Yakum-Yodko Narekevitch was successful in showing the difference in the Aura of a healthy person and a sick person by using high voltage and high frequency electric charges.

In 1939, Semyon Kirlian, without using any light source, passed electrical charge through living as well as non-living things and recorded them on film. Different light patterns were observed around them. This technique was called Corono-discharge photography or Kirlian photography. Only in 1960 details of this technique were published by Kirlian and his wife. It is the scientific proof of the existing 'electromagnetic field' in and around a human body called the Aura. The Aura is the 'invisible body' surrounding our physical body. This Aura consists of several layers which contain all the forms that the physical body has. In other words, it consists of all the five basic elements: Earth, Water, Fire, Air and Ether. Each layer is considered to be a level of higher vibrations but each layer appears different and has its own characteristics. Each layer of the Aura is associated with chakra, i.e. the first layer is associated with the first chakra, the second layer with the second chakra, and so on.

According to some scientists and healers, there are seven layers of Aura (Fig. 12) but more often four layers of Aura are talked about. These four layers of Aura surrounding the physical body are the Mental, Emotional, Intellectual and Spiritual layers. Only the physical body is visible, whereas the four layers which make up the Aura are invisible. Spiritually developed people tend to have a very bright clear Aura, especially around the head region. That is what is seen around the heads of the saints and holy people in their portraits made by artists.

The mental body, which is the first layer surrounding our physical body, is also a structured body. Normal colour of this layer is supposed to be yellow, but this colour changes, depending on the mental state of the person at a given time. Within this layer, one's thought forms can be seen. The thought forms get additional colours from the emotional level. The mixed colours of mental and emotional layers represent the person's emotion that is connected to the thought form.

The emotional layer around our body is the second Auric body and is associated with feelings. Clear and highly energized feelings such as love, excitement, joy or anger are bright and clear. The diffused feelings are dark. As the body gets energized with the help of meditations, these muddy, dark colours start becoming bright. To reach this layer, a person has to have unconditional love for fellow beings. When we show unconditional love for others, we have an open heart chakra, and this chakra connects us to fellow beings emotionally.

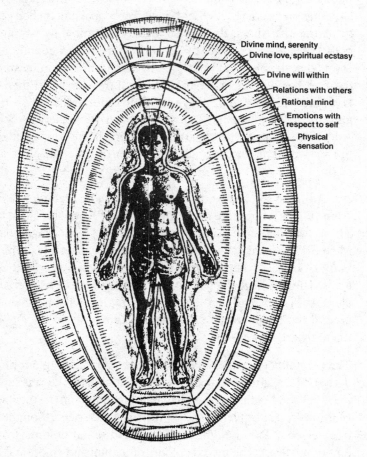

Divine mind, serenity
Divine love, spiritual ecstasy
Divine will within
Relations with others
Rational mind
Emotions with respect to self
Physical sensation

Fig. 12: *The Seven Levels of the Auric Field*

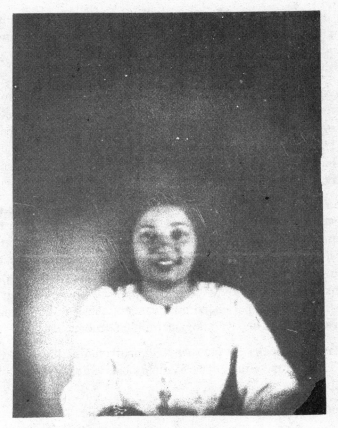

Fig. 13: *An Aura Photograph*

The intellectual layer of the body is the third Auric body. It creates an empty or negative space. It looks like a narrow oval shape and includes the entire energetic field consisting of chakras. When in a negative form, this layer is like that of a photograph negative. It helps our body to act intellectually when we deal with other people.

The final layer of the aura is the spiritual layer. It connects us, i.e. our physical body, with the universe. The layer varies from person to person, depending upon his spirituality. This can be expanded as the person becomes spiritual.

The Aura, as mentioned earlier, varies from person to person depending on age, sex, nature of the person and emotions. Even in case of an individual, his/her aura will not remain constant or same all the time. It varies from time to time depending on the mental and emotional state of the person. We can clean the aura by removing the blockages with the help of energy. This can make a person healthy, both physically and mentally.

The aura shows different colours. The colour of the aura tells the nature of the state of the person. The normal aura of a quiet, calm person suddenly may flash bright colours when the person is engaged in feelings or actions. Normally the body is surrounded by light blue colour, but around the head, it is yellow in colour (for highly spiritual people, it is white). Red is normally associated with anger.

Too many colours in the aura or the colours which are not in systematic layers i.e. of the colours appearing in the form of a number of feelings all at once, suggests he is in a confused state. Fear is shown by the light gray colour in the aura. Jealous people show dark green colour in their aura especially near solar plexus. Pink and white colours show happiness. From the energy field observations, experienced aura readers can see the connection between illness or psychological problems more clearly.

Writer and healer Barbara Ann Brennan studied the energy field and related the clinical energy field observations with emotional response.

General effects of colours are given below:

1. **Red :** It connects you to the earth. It gives strength, protects and charges the body. Good for all the organs near the first chakra.
2. **Orange :** Charges your sexual energy. Good for all organs near the second chakra. It makes the person creative.
3. **Yellow :** Gives mental clarity, cleans the mind of negative feelings and shows that you have a positive attitude towards the life.
4. **Green :** It brings balance and a feeling of fullness, good for the heart and lungs.
5. **Blue :** Brings peace, truth, and normally makes you speak truth.
6. **Indigo :** Opens spiritual perception, good for intuitive power.
7. **Violet :** It helps you to move towards spirituality.
8. **White :** It is a symbol of purity and peace. It brings spiritual expansion.

Conscious Levels of Mind

Kosha or Body	Psychological Dimension	Psychological State	Experienced as
Annamaya Kosha (Physical Body)	Conscious Mind	Wakeful Awareness	Awareness of physical body
Pranamaya Kosha (Mental Body)			Awareness of physiological functions, e.g. digestion, circulation
Manomaya Kosha (Emotional Body)	Subconscious Mind	Dreaming Awareness	Awareness of mental and emotional processes
Vigyanamaya Kosha (Intellectual Body)			Awareness of psychic and casual dimensions
Anandamaya Kosha (Spiritual body)	Unconscious Mind	Deep Sleep/Meditative Awareness	Homogeneous awareness; unconsciousness

Elements in the Body

The entire universe is a composition of five basic elements— Earth, Water, Fire, Air & Ether (Fig. 14). Our body is a mini universe which also consists of these basic elements. The prana also consists of the same elements.

These elements sustain us by providing energy. Our visible physical body and invisible aura is also made up of these five basic elements. A dynamic balance of matter and energy in relation to our body and mind gives more flexibility. Hence, it makes our life pleasant.

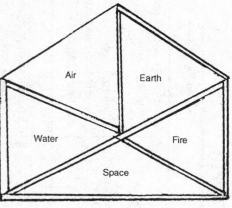

Fig. 14

Any disharmony between these elements (Fig. 14A, 14B & 14C) will cause our energies to dissipate, which causes ill health, stress, depression etc. To maintain a dynamic balance of these elements, we have to redirect our energies subjectively and objectively for happiness, success, wealth and prosperity of life.

S. No.	Element	Sense Organ	Function
1	Earth	Nose	Smell
2	Water	Tongue	Taste
3	Fire	Eyes	Sight
4	Air	Skin	Feeling
5	Ether	Ears	Sound

From the Supreme Being originated the ether which is similar to sound in nature. Sound is the link between perceptible and imperceptible. That which is beyond ether descends through sound into four grosser states, which are the touch, the sight, the taste and

58

Characteristics of the Five Basic Elements

Elements	Earth	Water	Fire	Air	Ether
Nature	Heavy	Cool	Hot	Erratic	Mixed
Quality	Weight, cohesion	Fluidity, contraction	Heat, Expansion	Motion, Movement	Diffused, space, giving
Colour	Yellow	White	Red	Blue/Grey	Black
Shape	Quadrangular	Crescent Moon	Triangular	Hexagonal	Blindudot
Chakra	Mooladhara	Swadhisthana	Manipura	Anahata	Vishuddha
Mantra	Lam	Vam	Ram	Ham	Gum
Tanmantra	Smell	Taste	Sight	Touch	Sound
Function in Body	Skin, Blood Vessels, Bone construction	All fluids of the body	Appetite, thirst, sleep	Expansion, contraction of muscles	Emotions, Passions
Location in Body	Thighs	Feet	Shoulder region	Navel region	Forehead
State of Mind	Ahamkara (ego)	Buddhi (Discrimination)	Manasa (thought, counter-thought)	Chitta (psychic content)	Pragya (intuition)
Kosha	Annamaya	Pranamaya	Manomaya	Vigyanamaya	Anandamaya
Prana Vayu	Apana	Prana	Samana	Udana	Vyana
Planet	Mercury	Moon and Venus	Sun and Mars	Saturn and Neptune	Jupiter
Direction	East	West	South	North	Middle and above

the smell. Ether is the basis of all formations and it is called the astral light. If we can work out with sound, automatically the four lower principles will be recognized. Since we live in the realm of sound we are nearer to that which is above the sound and that which is below the sound. From ether, air having the characteristic of touch came into existence. Then light characterized by form was produced. From light arose water representing taste. From water came out earth characterized by the smell.

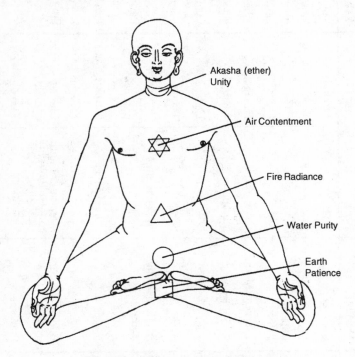

Akasha (ether) Unity

Air Contentment

Fire Radiance

Water Purity

Earth Patience

Fig. 14A: *Elements in the Body*

Ether has the quality of sound only. Air has two qualities i.e. sound & touch. Light or Fire is said to have triple qualities i.e. sound, touch & form. Water has got four qualities i.e. sound, touch, form and taste. Earth is endowed with five qualities i.e. sound, touch, form, taste and smell. The equilibrium of these elements on our planet is maintained forever.

Water evaporates from lakes, seas into the atmosphere with the help of heat (Fire), where it accumulates in the form of clouds, and the cool breeze (Air) condenses this into droplets to form rain. These five elements are needed by our body and mind are the cause of our existence.

Blue
The Absolute
The Ninth
Consciousness
Enlightenment

Wind Black
Nirvana
The five senses
Spiritual Body

Fire
Red
Enlightenment
Mind
Mental Body

Water
White
Practice
The " passionate mind"
Mental Body

Earth
Yellow
The Initial Awakening
The Store Consciousness
Physical/Etheric

Fig. 14B: *The Stupa and the Body*

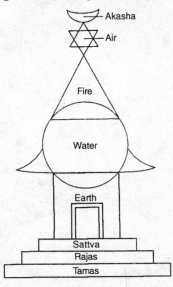

Akasha
Air
Fire
Water
Earth
Sattva
Rajas
Tamas

Fig. 14C: *The Stupa within the Body*

3. Understanding Reiki

Five Principles of Reiki

Dr. Mikao Usui, as stated earlier, has formed five principles to be followed by every practitioner of Reiki so that he/she can reduce the intensity of the level of negative emotions one has been withholding. These principles can enhance the positive attitude in a person. These principles have been shown in Fig. 15.

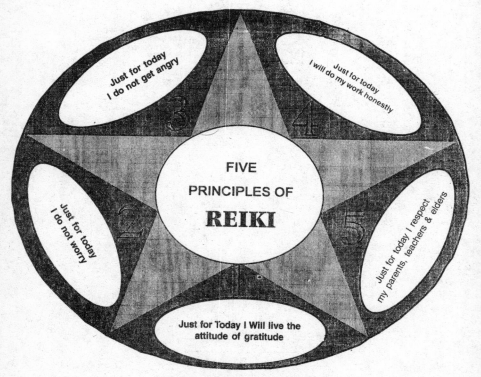

Fig. 15: *Five Principles of Reiki*

1. Just for Today I will Live with the Attitude of Gratitude

"A thankful heart is not only the greatest virtue, but the parent of all other virtues"

– Ciero.

Strictly speaking, gratitude is not meant for public or personal gratification and yet it strangely gladdens the heart of the receivers.

A great Roman statesman and orator, named Marcus Tillius Ciero lived in the first century before Christ. He was a very popular teacher and respected man in the society. He was well known among statesmen, officials, philosophers and other important people, but he maintained his simplicity. Once Ciero's students invited him for dinner. Though he avoided such invitations normally, as a special case he attended. Students were very happy with Ciero's presence. After the great dinner, he thanked everyone and finally went to the bearer and thanked him. He said, "Thank you, the food was wonderful, but it became tastier by your more wonderful service." Tears rolled down the cheeks of the slave, because nobody had thanked him before.

So before starting the Reiki practice, each day we always follow this principle of 'Attitude of Gratitude'.

I thank myself for being here, I thank Reiki for being here, I thank Dr. Mikao Usui for being here (one should feel his presence), I thank my Reiki master for being here, and so on. We can thank all those people to whom we want to express our gratitude.

We should be thankful to God that he gave us such a beautiful life. We can never be happy if we compare ourselves with people who are wealthier. Compare yourself with those who do not have enough to eat, enough to wear and no place to take shelter. You will realize how rich you are in all these respects.

We normally are not living with an attitude of gratitude because we are not satisfied with what we have. Not to be satisfied with what we have, seems to be part of human nature. We rarely like the present set of circumstances but appreciate those of others.

Once I read a story, which I would like to share with my readers.

When God started His creation, he was deciding the life span of all the animals. Man was sitting at the last, and by the time his turn came, only 25 years were left. He was very unhappy and said that at that age the real life starts. Then the ox sitting nearby was generous and gave 25 years from its lifespan. God did not have any objection. Still man was not happy and kept grumbling. This time the dog gave 25 years from its life span. Still man was unhappy. Next the owl gave 25 years from its life span. So man got an average life span of 100 years, but the original 25 years of his age is the best period. After that, between 25 and 50 years, he leads the life that of an ox, struggling for the family. The next 25 years from 50-75 years he leads the life like that of a dog, watching the house after his retirement, and from 75-100 years he is like an owl sitting at one place and is unable to see and move properly.

The attitude of gratitude is an inner state of being thankful for everything. The inner feeling is more important than mere saying the words.

2. Just for Today I will not Worry

Worry is the root cause of any disease. Worry leads to physical ailments like ulcer, headache, and mental diseases like depression. In many people, worry leads to stress. It is very easy to say not to worry, but very difficult to practise the same. Every person, these days, is exposed to occupational, environmental, mental, physical, emotional and dietary problems. These situations lead a person towards worry. The worry may be acute or chronic. The acute worry is sudden and lasts for a short period, whereas a chronic worry is a long-time worry, which is nagging. Chronic worry is dangerous. The best way to overcome worry is to train the mind in a proper way, because according to *Bhagawad Gita,* "Mind is the root cause of man's freedom from slavery of worldly shackle." When the mind accepts the circumstances, we are happy and when it doesn't, we are worried.

Once Sikh Guru Govind Singh went to the battlefield with his four sons and returned alone after defeating the Mughal army. His wife, who was waiting eagerly for her husband and four sons, asked the whereabouts of sons, but she could not get the reply for her repeated questioning. Then she realized that her sons will never return, and this led her to worry. She could not hold it. Tears rolling down, she kept worrying about her children. Finally, Guru Govind Singh said, "Our sons are immortal, consider our sons of our soil as our children. Please train your mind that way."

Normally, most of us worry — either brooding about the past or fearing about the future. This happens only because we normally do not live in the present. If you surrender yourself to the Supreme Being, you can release yourself from worry.

3. Just for Today I will not Get Angry

"Anybody can be angry, that is easy but to be angry with the right person and to the right degree and at the right time and for the right purpose, and in the right way, that is not within everybody's power and is not easy."

— Aristotle

"There are three gateways to hell leading to the ruin of the soul — lust, anger and greed. Therefore, one should abandon these three."

— Bhagawad Gita

"When anger comes, think of the consequences, it will soon subside."

— Confucius

A person normally gets angry when his ego is not satisfied, when the other person does not agree to what he said, when anything goes against his wishes or instructions. Whatever may be the reason, when anger is expressed, whatever may be the degree of anger, it creates an unpleasant situation, and more importantly, it even harms the body and mind of the angry person. Anger makes a person tense, causes hyperactivity of the adrenal glands, which increase the heartbeat, sugar level etc. All these changes utilize energy. So a person who gets angry very often loses a lot of energy. Besides, he spoils his relationship with others. Anger also affects his work power.

But at the same time, anger should never be suppressed, because suppressed anger also leads to diseases like skin irritation. Instead, a person should resolve his or her anger by different methods like going for a long walk when the situation is leading to an argument or misunderstanding. Doing physical exercises removes all the tensions of the mind and makes a person relaxed.

Lord Buddha always admonished his disciples and followers to restrain from getting angry. The best way to do so is to see good in everything that appears to be harmful. If you cannot control your anger, you act like a driver who does not have control on his powerful vehicle, which results in the destruction of his own self.

Once Lord Buddha was taking his disciples to a village, which was notorious for its ill-tempered, arrogant people. He told his disciples to remain cheerful even if the villagers do not welcome them thinking that they have not abused. Even if they abuse you, remain cheerful thinking that they have not beaten you. Even if they beat you, remain thinking that they have not killed you. Even if they kill you, remain cheerful as they can never destroy your spirit.

4. Just for Today I will do My Work Honestly
Honesty is Quality of Heart, Head and Soul.

"An honest man is the noblest work of God."   — **Pope**

"The bread earned by the sweat of brow is thrice blessed and it is far sweeter than the tasteless loaf of idleness."
— **Alfred Craw Quill**

Duty if not performed is bad and sinful, but duty performed without honesty is worse and more sinful. To earn as much money as possible in as little time as possible is a common feature of the society for all times. So that pleasure of honest work and honest money is lost.

Shri M. Visweswaraiya, world renowned Indian engineer, once went to the USA where he had to lecture before the faculty of engineering. Due to lack of time, he gave all technical details to a professional writer to prepare his lecture. He was very happy to see the script, which was prepared very well. He gave $8 as his fee and one more additional dollar as gratification money to the writer's secretary as the writer was not present at that time.

The next day the writer returned the dollar saying, "It is not earned out of my sweat. If I form such a habit I will miss the real pleasure of earning the money by my own perseverance."

5. Just for Today I will Respect my Parents, Teachers and Elders

"Selfless service to humanity is the foremost duty of the youth."
— **Bhagawan Swaminarayan**

"Honour the guru! He has shown us the way to perfection,"

Alexander did not obey his teacher's words and crossed the river first. Aristotle was more surprised than hurt because it never happened before. On reaching the other bank, when Aristotle enquired, Alexander said, "Sir, your life is more precious than mine. The world will have many more Alexanders, not another Aristotle."

The same way, Aruni, who went to inspect the mud wall of his teacher's field, found that the walls were getting washed away. As he could not seal it with mud chunks, he placed himself there carefully to stop the damage.

These examples show great respect for the guru. To show love and respect for others is to love and respect ourselves.

Concepts of Reiki

Reiki is a method of healing oneself with the help of cosmic energy, which is called 'Universal Life Force Energy'. The other way to understand Reiki is that "It is a high level, deep-rooted meditation, wherein we invoke cosmic energy in our body through the chakras to energize our physical, mental, emotional, intellectual, and spiritual bodies." This energy, when absorbed into the body, relieves us from all the negativity, and hence from all the diseases. The primitive man lived happily because he lived with the cosmic energy made up of five basic elements — Earth, Water, Fire, Air and Ether. However, today we are living in a world of pollution, tension, worry and pressures. Though every person is a born Reiki channel and is free to absorb this energy, most of us are unable to do so as we are not aware of it.

Sometimes the energy is insufficient as we spend most of our energy (80 per cent) within the brain because of our tensions and problems. Reiki helps us to take the energy and utilize it in our body as and when required. It has no side effects unlike the use of modern medicines. Tha does not mean we should totally discard or ignore modern medicin e. To find out the level of thyroxin in thyroid, level of sugar in diabetes, one needs to consult the doctor. But, applying Reiki is of great help when we know the problem. Modern medicine has its limitations, as the treatment is external. Hence, alternative approaches to health and healing are necessary especially in relation to chronic diseases. Modern medicine may give immediate relief, but normally it suppresses the actual disease. Reiki helps uprooting the problems. It is the simplest method of healing the body, mind and spirit.

Sometimes, Reiki appears to fail in a particular case but that is not due to Reiki. It is due to the person who is receiving the Reiki. Some people enjoy their illness, i.e. they take advantage of their illness. People, who do not want to get better or come out of their illness for some reason or the other, are difficult persons to be healed through Reiki. In that case, first the mental attitude of the person has to be changed by counselling and then Reiki should be given. Normally old people, children and sick people want other's attention. So, as long as the diseased person gets attention, he does not want to get well.

We know a lady, who attended our seminar. She used to get severe headache in the evening and she used to become well by night. Everyday her husband used to come home by 5.30 p.m. in the evening, who otherwise never came home before 9 p.m. Now, the reason behind her headache was loneliness, and she wanted her husband's company. After she attended our classes with the help of counselling and constant Reiki treatment, she became interested in Reiki. She was regularly attending our seminars and became our assistant. When she was involved in Reiki, it acted as an occupational therapy, changing the complexion of her life, in addition to ridding her of headache.

The person's attitude, belief in himself/herself & faith in Reiki are important. If a person does not have any faith and is forced into

Reiki, the healing takes a longer time, say, till the mentality of the person is changed. In such cases, distant healing is helpful so that slowly the person's nature becomes acceptable. Reiki helps in cleansing process. This cleansing process may be at the physical or emotional level. At the physical level, Reiki removes the toxic substances from the body and at the mental and emotional levels, the negativities can be eliminated.

Reiki can cure any disease from simple type of indigestion, headache, fever, to complicated diseases such as heart problems, arthritis, diabetes, kidney problems, severe back problems etc. This is not something new, it was practised in the earlier days and was clearly mentioned in the Vedas. In the Vedas, importance was given to the dictum: 'our health is in our hands', as is clear from the following excerpt:

अयं में हस्तो भगवानयं में भगवत्तुर।
अयं में विश्व भेषजोऽयं शिषांथिदर्शना।
ऋग्वेद 10.60.12 अथर्ववेद 4.13.6

Doubts always arose about the existence of the cosmic energy, because one cannot see anything concrete about it. Though many people can feel the energy flowing and the warmth of the hands, others are skeptical about it as they cannot feel it. When we breathe in and out, we do not feel but we know that the air present in our atmosphere is taken in and oxygen present in that is utilized by our body. Without this oxygen, living organisms cannot live. Hence, it is called "Prana Vayu."

Similarly, the cosmic energy present in the universe is essential for our body. Our body takes this energy through our chakras. We do not feel, because we are not conscious of it. Because this energy is essential for living, it is called "Prana Shakti."

Reiki Positions for Treatment of Self & Others

Attitude of Gratitude

Front of the body: 1. Eyes, 2. Temples, 3. Ears, 4. Forehead/ Back of the Head, 5. Both hands at the back of the Head, 6. Throat,

7. Thyroid and Thymus, 8. Heart Chakra, 9. Solar Plexus, 10. Liver, 11. Lung Tips, 12. Spleen & Pancreas, 13. Hara Chakra, 14. Ovaries/ Spermatic cords (Root Chakra), 15. Knees, 16. Ankles, 17. Feet Soles.

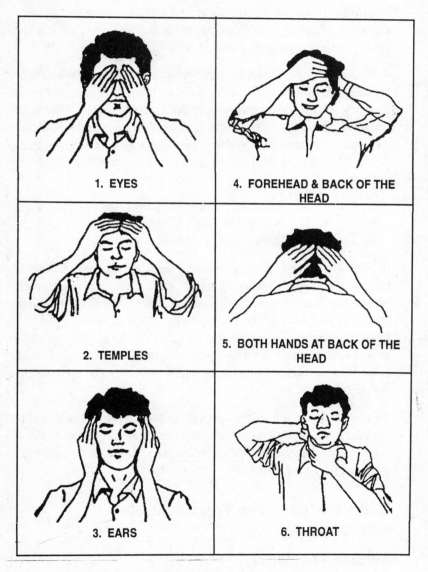

Reiki Positions for Treatment of Self & Others

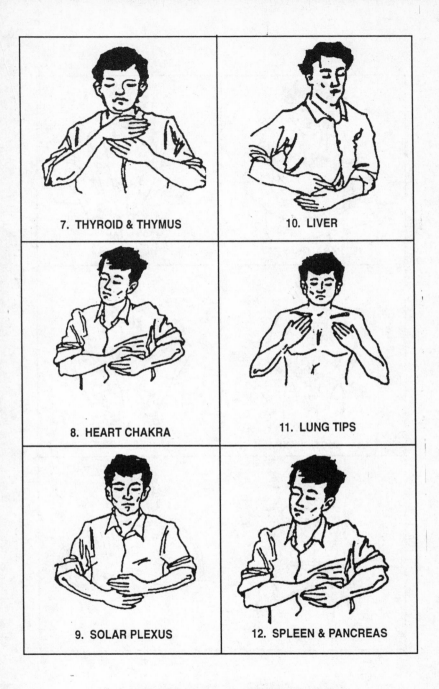

7. THYROID & THYMUS

10. LIVER

8. HEART CHAKRA

11. LUNG TIPS

9. SOLAR PLEXUS

12. SPLEEN & PANCREAS

Reiki Positions for Treatment of Self & Others

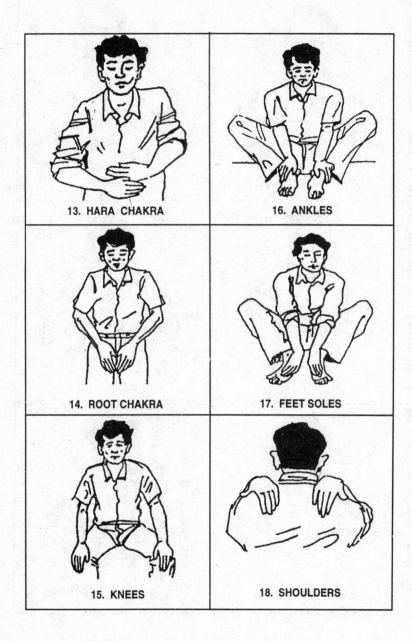

13. HARA CHAKRA

16. ANKLES

14. ROOT CHAKRA

17. FEET SOLES

15. KNEES

18. SHOULDERS

Reiki Positions for Treatment of Self & Others

Back of the body: 18. Shoulders, 19. Thyroid and Thymus, 20. Heart Chakra, 21. Solar Plexus, 22. Kidneys, 23. Hara Chakra, 24. Base of the Spine (Root Chakra).

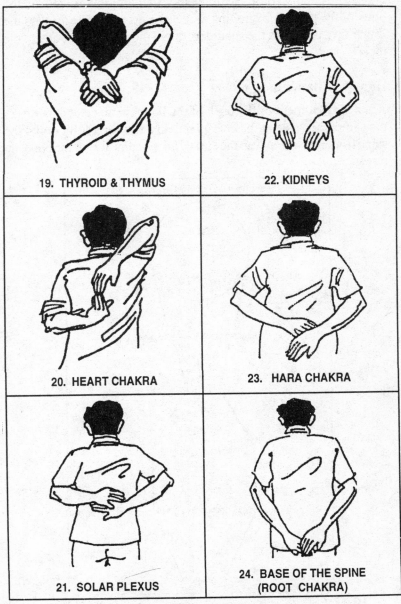

19. THYROID & THYMUS

22. KIDNEYS

20. HEART CHAKRA

23. HARA CHAKRA

21. SOLAR PLEXUS

24. BASE OF THE SPINE (ROOT CHAKRA)

Reiki Positions for Treatment of Self & Others

Spiraling

On completion of the treatment of the front of the body, draw anti-clockwise energy spirals with the index and middle fingers on the body of the patient, beginning at the armpits down the arms to the finger tips, and from the shoulders down the side of the body to the toes.

Energy Balancing

After the treatment of the back of the body, balance the energy in the spine, then sweep the energy quickly and forcefully down the spine (for diabetics, sweep the energy up the spine, i.e. in the opposite direction.)

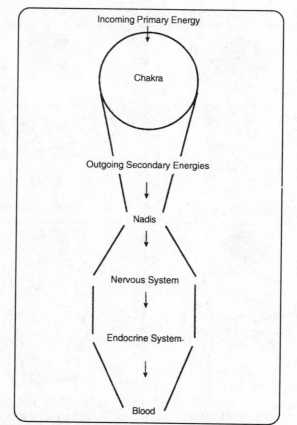

Metabolic Path of incoming Primary Energy or Reiki Energy
(Pran Shakti)

Reiki II: Distance Healing

(a) Imagine that you are there with the person receiving the healing, and do the healing. To speed up the process, you can also imagine yourself with several pairs of extra arms!

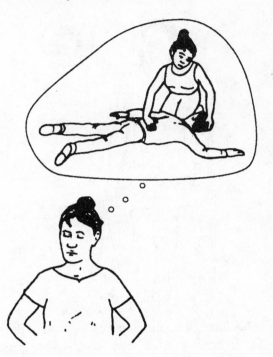

(b) Imagine the person/animal/plane shrunk small enough to heal in your hands.

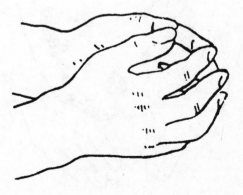

(c) Imagine your knee is the receiver's body, and do the healing. Focus on the person receiving the healing. Use the left knee for the person's front, and the right knee for the back of her body. Your knee is her head, your thigh her torso, and your hip her legs and feet.

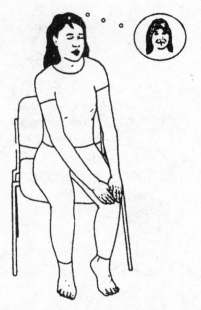

(d) Use a teddy bear, doll, pillow or photograph of the person as a surrogate. Do the healing on the bear, then imagine giving the healed bear to the person receiving the distance treatment. Tell her, "Take what you can use from the bear."

Reiki Certification

Reiki I: Reiki is a very simple technique that does not require any special talent and tools. Even children can learn it easily and can apply it. First degree training gives 20 per cent power transfer, which is sealed in the student. First degree is usually taught in a two-day workshop. During this time the student is given an idea about the history of Reiki, i.e. the story of Dr. Mikao Usui who rediscovered Reiki. The basic hand positions are also taught for self treatment and for treating others. Altogether four attunements are given — two on the first day and two on the second day. These attunements make the person feel the Reiki energy by increasing the heat, tingling or pulsations in the hands. In addition, several exercises like partner treatment, group treatment (figure given below) etc., and meditations like centring are also taught. At the end of the session after clearing the doubts which may be expressed by the participants, first degree certificates are awarded. People are encouraged to treat self, relatives, friends, etc.

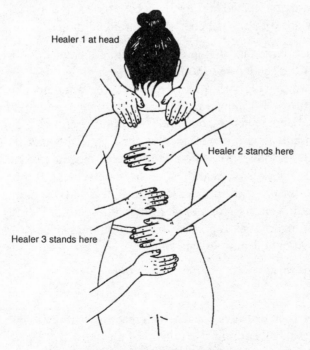

Healer 1 at head

Healer 2 stands here

Healer 3 stands here

Group Healing (The Big H)

Reiki II: This is not awarded until at least 30 days after the first degree certification. Reiki first degree deals with only touch healing, but after the second degree, a Reiki channel can send healing beyond time and space, with a four times higher level of energy than Reiki I. First degree attunements help in intensifying the energy level in the physical body whereas second degree attunements help in intensifying the energy level in the etheric body. This attunement stimulates the Ajna chakra by which the intuitive power increases. In Reiki II, a connection is made between a person who is sending Reiki and the person who is receiving it. This is done with the help of a key of the first symbol called bridge making symbol. The second symbol is used to remove the obstacles on the way and to remove blockages in the Aura and the physical body of the patient. This symbol acts as a block removal symbol. Finally, a third symbol is used to increase the energy level. This symbol is called energy intensifying symbol. So, distance Reiki is done with the help of symbols. These symbols are the symbols which are referred to in the *'Lotus Sutras'* and are very sacred and secretive. Though these symbols are published in some books by some authors, I would not like to discuss them, as I consider them to be sacred.

One must remember that in distant healing a connection is made between the sender and the receiver like a coded wireless radio transmitter and receiver. In the second degree, attunement is given along with the three keys or symbols and absentee healing is taught. A second degree certificate is presented at the end of the session and participants are encouraged to send Reiki beyond time and space. In our class, we encourage our participants to give Reiki energy to orphans & destitutes in our country, and to the people who are suffering from diseases like cancer, AIDS, and also to unforeseen victims like war victims, and cyclone victims. The students are advised to practise for a minimum period of 90 days for detoxification and self cleansing.

Reiki III: The third degree is divided into two parts *viz.* 3A & 3B.

3A: This degree allows you to accelerate the treatment time, deals with mental and emotional problems of the patient.

3B: This degree allows a person to teach Reiki and confer the first and second degree through power transfers. It can be conferred only by an individual who has received the special Reiki keys rediscovered by Dr. Mikao Usui. The person, who is interested in 3B, should be totally dedicated and committed to teach the Usui system of natural healing.

Once initiated into first degree, anyone can heal, and it does not require special talents nor it can be done wrongly. The more the healer uses Reiki, the stronger it becomes. Reiki will never leave one sealed during attunements, except if he attempted to misrepresent the process by claiming to teach and give power transfer without getting the third degree certification. Faith, unconditional love, devotion towards self healing and to heal others who are in distress with affection, are the qualities required for any healer, who wishes to attain higher levels of perfection and to improve one's personality at all the five different levels — Physical, Mental, Emotional, Intellectual & Spiritual — in an integrated and holistic manner.

On Being Certified

Now that you are a Reiki master, you realize anytime you touch someone or something, the universal life force energy turns on.

Your Reiki is the Midas touch of healing. Yet don't be disillusioned even if after your first-degree certification you occasionally experience a physical or emotional distress. Reiki is not Nirvana or heaven or omnipresent bliss ; though compared to what some people have chosen to suffer and how segments of the medical community treat (or can't treat) certain ailments, it may seem that way to the healed client.

Disease and subsequent ailments will remain an aspect of mass consciousness for some time to come in this world. So when you find yourself in a lowered energy state, remember Reiki works on you too! And don't hesitate to request the aid of other Reiki therapists to magnify the universal life energy flow in you. The increase of universal life energy through Reiki affects your emotional health more than physical health.

Reiki is an impetus to spiritual growth. Follow the happenings of life, they will lead you to places and people that will promote inner growth. Focal points of priorities of living will be altered. More and more you will find a quiet honesty about your actions and your lifestyle. Be prepared for growth and spiritual healing.

So use your hands...in mixing foods, vitalizing water, and healing in all its myriad forms.

Your touch will feel good to others, too. Go, hug lots of people!

Be prepared to experience growth, consciousness expansion and spiritual strength.

Who to Treat

First, treat yourself. You are a Reiki expert and can be in as perfect health as your ego will allow yourself to be.

Second, treat family members. Normally, the family unit will have provided you with many benefits, and transmitting the health of Reiki is an excellent way to complete the exchange.

Third, consider treating anyone who asks. Asking is important, because Reiki is a system based on intent. The prospective client should express his intent for health by requesting the treatment.

Naturally, if the person is in coma, or an infant, or someone whose family asked for the healing or someone for whom you are responsible, it is appropriate to do Reiki.

By stating in your mind, "You are free to accept or reject this healing as you will", you release the will of the client and do not impose your will upon them.

Be cautious in treating an accident victim you don't know. In that case, it is legally advisable not to say anything about your healing ability. Simply attempt to administer Reiki in an inconspicuous manner which fortunately is very easy with Reiki.

Speaking of infants, don't think babies, even foetuses, are too young to receive treatments. "Reiki just works Zing-O on babies", affirms Samdahl enthusiastically. "They have no barriers whatsoever. They are wide open to God's love. And that's what healing is; God loving us."

Persons hospitalized or under conventional medical care, can also be treated with Reiki.

If the patient takes medication, instruct him to regularly consult his physician because as Reiki rebalances his body, the prescribed dosage might have to be lessened to avoid overdoses.

Do not diagnose illness and prescribe medicines unless you are an MD. Suggest rather than direct. Simply state what you'd do if you had the condition perceived, giving the patient the responsibility to assess its merits for himself.

It is also important to remember that you should never feel forced or obligated to heal someone, or guilty for not taking the time to heal whenever and wherever requested.

Don't forget pets, animals and plants, they also have universal life energy, and Reiki works for them too.

"The big bonus with Reiki is that when you are treating someone else, you are receiving a healing at the same time", says Mrs. Samdahl.

"One is never tired nor depleted after giving a treatment since we are using universal life energy, not our own."

While healing is generally thought of in terms of living creatures, this universal life energy pervades all creations.

Therefore, you can consider applying Reiki in some rather unorthodox healing situations. WHAT to treat can become as vital a consideration as WHO to treat.

Treating Infants, Plants, Animals, Food and Assorted Odds and Ends

Pregnant women enjoy Reiki treatments because they help to alleviate some of the minor and major complaints of pregnancy such as morning sickness in the first trimester, and later, lower back pain. Reiki also helps to soothe women as emotions begin to fluctuate due to the large amount of hormones being released in the system. The infant itself appears to enjoy Reiki. During the time my sister was pregnant, the treatments seemed to energize her body, baby's feet would start to kick and little elbows would poke out. Also, the baby would tend to change positions more often during treatments, while there was still enough free space to move. We used Reiki on my sister during the entire birth process, and treated my niece immediately after birth.

Reiki practitioners, who are involved with gardening, are well aware of the benefits that plants derive from being treated. Seeds that are treated before being planted, tend to grow into healthier plants than those which are not treated. Hold them between the palms of your hands and treat them as long as they draw energy. Seed sprouts in the earth can be treated by holding your hands just above them. Regular treatments given to your vegetable garden help to produce an abundance of vital healthy plants. Flowers and shrubs do very well too when treated with Reiki. Blossoms tend to proliferate, and the growth of shrubs is accelerated. Cut flowers tend to last longer when supported with Reiki, and house plants also react with beneficial results.

Much has been written about the secret life of plants. Scientific tests have been done to show how plants react to our emotions and to music. It has also been found that talking to plants helps to aid in their healthy development. The great success of the Findhorn community in Northern Scotland is world renowned. In a very barren wind-swept coastal area, a group of people have successfully turned an otherwise unedernourished land into a prolific garden paradise. By incorporating the help of nature spirits, they have successfully tuned in with their environment and have overcome otherwise insurmountable difficulties to produce a lavish abundance of plant growth. Following the example of Findhorn and similar other communities we can accomplish otherwise impossible tasks on the planet by communicating with the elements of nature.

Second degree Reiki practitioners might consider sending treatments to the elementals of certain plants to help them in their work on the Earth. The cooperation between humans and nature writs may result in the rejuvenation of the entire ecological system.

Animals are appreciative recipients of Reiki energy, and most often become very calm and relaxed while treated. Occasionally, you will find a rare animal who rejects the energy, and that must be respected. The average animal, however, will experience the same benefits that humans do. The fact that animals are healed with Reiki treatments, tends to prove that the belief system has little effect on the outcome of the healing, although faith in any cure does help.

Animal anatomy is very similar to human anatomy, so when treating a specific organ in an animal's body, you can judge its position fairly easily by its placement in your body. Also, as with treating humans, special attention should be given to areas which draw larger amounts of energy. Covering the endocrine system, whenever possible, is also recommended.

If an animal is restless, or it seems dangerous to treat with hands on, absentee healing can be utilized. Patting an animal before treatment is one way to soothe it. You can then follow your intuition in the placement of your hands. Altogether, you will find Reiki a very practical tool for maintaining the health of your pets.

Reiki can be used to energize an assortment of objects. Crystals have already been mentioned. Gem stones and jewellery are also the possibilities, along with an assortment of other objects. We must keep in mind that all matter is vibration at different levels of density — that everything on the physical plane is composed of universal life force energy in different phases of evolution. As all matter is vibration, Reiki can penetrate anything, much like the etheric substance of your body which permeates your environment. It is also possible to clear an environment such as hotel room with Reiki energy, to remove any negative etheric substance.

On the more mundane level, cars and boats can also be treated. These objects actually tend to take on the etheric energy of their owners and become affected by their moods. Have you ever noticed that when you are in negative or "down" cycle, your car tends to break down, or you blow out a sail? Boaters are especially aware of how their boats tend to take on an actual personality. Machines act as our mirrors as they become permeated with our energy over time. They become the anuma to our anumus or the anumus to our anuma. When the two are not in harmony, Reiki treatments are called for, because they can help you to avoid undesirable breakdowns and mechanical mishaps.

Finally, it should be mentioned that food can be enhanced by treating it with Reiki. In most countries around the world, people tend to eat an excessive amount of cooked or "dead" foods. In America alone, the average person eats 75% cooked food and only 25% raw food. In countries with the most centenarians, such as Russia, Bulgaria, the Hunzas in India, and some of the Mayan cultures, the people eat about a 73% raw food diet and 27% cooked food diet. The raw food provides live enzymes which keep the body young and healthy and prevent the deterioration which causes quick aging in most of the human race. A raw food diet is an important factor in health. When you are in situations which prevent you from obtaining the correct amount of raw, live foods, you can enhance your cooked food with the universal life force energy or Reiki. By just holding your hands above your plate, you can treat your food and afterwards, also treat your belly to aid in the process of digestion.

As we have seen in this chapter, all matter is composed of the universal life force at different levels of vibration. Reiki, which is channelled and intensified form of this energy, can be used to energize not only living, breathing life forms, but also "solid" matter. You are encouraged to allow your imagination free reign and to use your intuition to explore the endless possibilities.

How to Treat

Your instructor will cover this topic in great detail. Here are some basic points:

- First create an environment as quiet, comfortable and soothing as possible for treatment.

In the home, set aside a room or designate a small area to be regularly used for client treatment. This "Reiki space" will become familiar (and thus psychologically comfortable) for clients who require successive treatments and also becomes charged with the nature of Reiki itself, thereby facilitating the healing experience.

Wear comfortable clothing that won't interfere with the treatment positions.

For male patients: remove glasses, vest, jacket, tie and belt, shoes, have the pockets emptied.

For female patients: remove glasses, shoes, belt, scarves and jewellery around the neck; no girdles or tight pantyhose.

No terribly snug pants in either case.

- Most treatments by first-degree practitioners are hands-on. Remote or absentee healing is taught in second-degree Reiki.

However, occasionally it may not be possible to touch the patient directly due to severe skin infection/lesions or second/third degree burns, or thick layers of clothing or plaster cast. Or you may wish to treat an infant and don't want to disturb his shallow sleep.

Know that Reiki finish does require direct physical contact with the skin, though.

- Insist on proper hygiene for yourself, just as you would expect from any medical professional.

Always have clean hands, washing hands with soap before treatment and afterwards for 20-30 seconds in cool running water to break the energy flow is required. If in an emergency situation water is not available, form the hands in the "prayer" position with fingertips together and press firmly for 30 seconds.

- Place a box of tissues and a sheet or blanket within easy reach.

The tissues are for eye treatment and certain ailments; the covers for the client's comfort.

- Have the client lie down, if possible, so that gravity can aid in pulling Reiki into his body.

85

Place a pillow under his head; another under his back, another under his knees to relieve pressure on the lower back. Employ the sheet or light blanket if the client complains of chills.

And don't neglect to ensure your own needs either. Remember the comfort of yourself and the client is the next most important thing to Reiki itself during a treatment.

- Make sure the client's feet are not crossed; this tends to 'short circuit' the energy flow.

- Tell the client he may feel worse after the first or second treatment, either due to severe imbalance in an organ (or the body generally) or because you may stop treatment just as the illness has been brought back from the chronic stage to its acute stage before eventual release.

If this happens, a minimum three, preferably four, consecutive daily treatments will be required unless healing takes place after the first or second treatment.

"The disease must return from where it came", is the basic Reiki tenet.

- Ask the client about ailments irritated by touching; also enquire about any major surgery.

- "Notify people what you're going to do", says Samdahl with a grin, "so you don't scare them to death."

- "Treat HEAD, FRONT and BACK, and hold anything that hurts and anything can't go wrong."

"Think of the front (neck to waist) as the 'Master Motor' of the body."

- Keep your fingers together, otherwise energy is scattered. Curve the fingers just slightly to rest upon the contours of the body rather than making them stiff and flat.

- Begin by spending 8-10 minutes on each position.

As you practise Reiki and your bio-sensory system becomes more attuned to the universal life energy, you will sense a varying rhythmic

86

rise and fall of energy under your hands. Your power to channel Reiki will also increase, and treatment time will shorten. Extremely diseased centres will probably need prolonged placements.

Your hands will tell you through its sinusodial pattern when to break. Do so at the end of the first cycle of peak-to-ebb flow, just as the energy is about to rise again. That completes one energy cycle for that particular organ of the body drawing in the most Reiki.

Each period will differ, depending on the organ and its condition.

- If the client has organs missing due to surgery, treat as if they are present anyway. Reiki can help set up an energy pattern within the body to balance the body as if that organ were physically present, and will release adhesions if they exist.

- A cold spot indicates a dysfunctioning organ or impaired circulation. Hold the area until warm.

- "There is no such thing as a partial treatment because the body is all linked in, as you all know."

For instance, if a person has diabetic blindness you are not going to cure the eyes until you cure the pancreas — because the pancreas is what manufactures insulin and a lack of insulin is what creates diabetes and diabetes is what can create diabetic blindness, etc. So, until the pancreas is healed, nothing is going to happen to diabetic blindness.

- So besides emergency situations, always give the whole body treatment before focusing on particular ailments for additional Reiki. As you are giving your time, the client should be equally agreeable to give his time for a proper treatment. The client has given you the authority by requesting a Reiki treatment, so be firm about what you know must be done.

If partial treatment must be done, treat the solar plexus and adrenals. (This is also good for energy revitalization and "bringing things back to life".)

- Reiki is pulled through the body at a rate corresponding to the need of the client.

- The more the energy needed to regenerate, rejuvenate and revitalize the injured body, the longer the healing will generally take.

- "At the end of 10 minutes, almost every organ has all the Reiki it needs." Samdahl instructs as a guideline.

- **TEAM TREATMENTS:** Divide points on FRONT and BACK positions. Treat front simultaneously, then treat back simultaneously.

Simultaneous treatment on the torso and head is also very beneficial.

Also when possible, have one healer hold the soles of the client's feet as a means to boost his energy field.

Reiki Finish: When the client has accepted all the Reiki needed at one session, conclude his treatment with the Reiki Finish; it's like "icings on the cake."

a. On completion of the treatment of the front of the body, draw anticlockwise energy spirals with the index and middle fingers on the body of the patient — beginning at the shoulders down the arms to the finger tips and from the shoulders down along the side of the body to the tip of the toes.

b. Have the client lie on his stomach and bare his back.

c. Put one hand on neck, feel the throat chakra. Keep the hand one inch above the body.

d. Put the other hand on root chakra & feel the energy of the root chakra. Keep the hand one inch above the body.

e. Bring both the hands together in the centre i.e. on solar plexus & heart chakra and balance the energy.

f. If the client has no diabetic tendency, form a 'V' with two fingers and place them at the base of the neck and pull down along the spine.

   For pancreatic conditions, use the above 'up' motion stroke from the base of the spine to the base of the neck, "for this cleanses the blood".

g. Wash your hands again, or press your fingertips together for 30 seconds to close down the energy flow.

The Reiki treatment is now complete.... yet the effect of the Reiki on the cells and energy flow on the body does not end with the treatment, but continues to build and balances the cells and system.

Reiki can be given to a person by a group of Reiki Channels or healers. This helps in reducing the time required to impart a full body treatment. It is not advantageous to have more than four persons in a group treatment because the time cannot be reduced below 21 minutes. Given below are body positions to be treated by each healer in a group treatment situation.

Case 1 : (2 persons treating) 39 minutes

1st person :   Points Nos. 1 to 7, (10), 18, 19, (20)

2nd person :   Points Nos. 8, 9, 11 to 17, 21 to 24.

Case 2 : (3 persons treating) 27 minutes

1st person :   Points 1 to 6, 18 & (19)

2nd person :   Points 7 to (11), 20 (21)

3rd person :   Points 12 to 17, 22 to 24

Case 3 : (4 persons treating) 21 minutes

1st person :   Points 1 to 5, (18)

2nd person :   Points 8 to 10, (13), 19 & 20

3rd person :   Points 6, 7, 11, (12), 21 & 22

4th person :   Points 14, (15) to 17, 23 & 24

Note: The bracketed numbers have to be given energy for 6 minutes.

"**Truth Never Dies:** The ages come and go,
The mountains wear away, the stars retire,
Destruction lays earth's mighty cities low,
And empires, states and dynasties expire,
But caught and handed onward by the
Wise : **Truth Never Dies**"
COPERNICUS

Hands

— giving and receiving holding on the reality
— reaching goals
— fear of action

Forearm

— means of attaining goals
— fear of inferiority

Elbow

— connects the strength of the upper arms to the action of the forearm

Upper back

— (particularly between the shoulder blades), we carry stored anger

Lower back

— junction between lower and upper body movement
— men store a lot here due to the storing of emotions in the blockage

Gluterus muscles

— holding in emotions — not releasing and letting go
— anal blockage

Abductors

— inner thigh
— contain sexually charged issues

Ankles

— create balance

Arms

— express the heart centre, love
— enable us to move and connect in the external world

Upper arm

— strength to act
— fear of being discouraged

Shoulders

— where we carry the weight of the world
— fear of responsibility
— women store a lot here

Back

— where we store all our unconscious emotions and excess tension

Pelvis

— seal of Kundalini energy
— root of basic survival needs and actions

Hamstrings

— self control issues
— letting go

Lower leg

— enables movement towards goals
— fear of action

Nose

— related to heart (coloration and bulbousness)
— sense and smell, sexual response
— self recognition

Mouth

— survival issues
— how we take in nourishment, security
— capacity to take in new ideas

Forehead

— intellectual expression

Neck

— thought and emotions come together
— stiffness is due to withheld statements

Arms and hands

— are extensions of heart centre
— express love and emotion

Solar Plexus (diaphragm)

— power issues
— emotional control issues
— power wisdom centre

Genitals

— related to root chakra containing Kundalini
— survival issues
— fear of life

Knees

— fear of death
— fear of death of the old-self or ego
— fear of change

Face

— expresses the various "makes" of our personality
— shows how we "face" the world

Eyes

— show how we see the world
— nearsighted is more withdrawn
— farsighted is less inner oriented
— windows of the soul

Brow

— intuitive centre
— emotional expression

Ears

— our capacity to hear
— have acupuncture points for every area of the body

Jaw

— tension indicates blockage of emotional and verbal communication
— fear or ease of expression

Chest	**Thigh**
— relationship issues	— personal strength
— heart and love emotions	— trust in one's own abilities
— respiration and circulation	— fear of strength

Abdomen	**Feet**
— seal of the emotions	— show if we are grounded
— contains our deepest feelings	— connected with reaching our goals
— centre of sexuality	
— digestive system	— fear of completion

Different Techniques of Using Reiki

For Treating Self:

Full Body (30 Days Self-purification): This is done from the day the seminar is over. It will require a minimum of 72 mins. (@ 3 mins./point for 24 points). The procedure for this is:

- Attitude of Gratitude: To start or restart after interruption. Close eyes, fold hands & say these words:

  I thank myself < self name > that I am here

  I thank Reiki that she is here

  I thank Dr. Mikao Usui that he is here

  I thank my parent's Guru, personal God etc. that they are here

  I thank < Partner's name > that he/she is receiving energy (if treating someone else)

- 17 Points on Front Body: This will take 51mins. @ 3 mins./points

- 7 Points on Back Body: Done after turning over. This will take 21 mins. @ 3 mins./point

- End: Wash hands or press fingertips together firmly for 1/2 minute to stop energy flow

Continue for a longer duration if required.

For Treating Others:

- **Full Body:** This is done as detailed above for a minimum of three days. The duration can be increased if required. Do front body. After front body is complete, do energy balancing.

- **Spirals:** Draw anti-clockwise spirals from shoulder to fingers and from armpits to feet on both sides of the body with first two fingers of one hand. Do back body. After back body is complete, do energy balancing.

- **Energy Balancing:** Place hands one inch over neck, back & root chakra back. Feel the energy by moving hands around a little. Then bring hands slowly together on heart back keeping them above the body & lift the hands up.

- **Stroking:** With a 'V' made from first two fingers of the hand, stroke down firmly from neck back to root chakra back three times (Stroke up from root chakra back to neck back for diabetes patients.)

- **Direct Spot:** This is for points other than the chakras and is done in addition and after the partial body treatment. The duration is 3 minutes or more as required.

Note: a) While shifting hands from one point to another, do not lift both hands simultaneously off the body. First shift one hand and then the other.

b) Do not wear metal articles or jewellery as they tend to sap energy.

c) If a body area cannot be touched directly, Reiki can be given from a distance of 1" above it.

4. Concept of Chakras & Healing

Light Circle

Have particulars of persons who need healing (name, age, location, disease), before starting the meditation.

- Sit straight and relax.
- Hold hands in a circle, left hand shows up and right hand shows down.
- Sit comfortably.
- Breathe deeply 3 times and relax.
- Imagine a ray of bright light coming from above and flowing through your Crown chakra into your body.
- Fill your body with this light.
- Let the energy flow in your circle.
- Take it with your left hand, let it stream through your body and give it to your neighbour on the right.
- Now open your Heart chakra and let the light flow out into the middle and fill your circle with this light.
- Fill this room with this light.
- Fill this whole house/building with this bright white light.
- Fill this city with this light.
- Fill our whole country with this light.
- Fill our planet Earth with this light, love and peace.
- We send light, love, peace & Reiki to (city or country), and see the people living together in peace and love.

Repeat the following for all Names in the list.

- We send light, love, healing and Reiki to (Name of the 1st person in the list) and see him/her totally healthy and joyful.

- Repeat after me (Name of the person) is healed.

Chakra Balancing

- For 30 days give full body treatment to yourself (all 24 points). For each point give 3 minutes. This can be done in two or three sittings.

- If you can continue full body treatment for long, that is much better. If you cannot do full body then do Chakra Balancing as follows:

– One palm on back of the forehead, the other palm on the **Root Chakra (Mooladhara Chakra).**

– Next, after 6/9 minutes, move the upper palm to front part of the forehead, lower palm from Muladhara area to navel area/**Hara Chakra (Swadhisthana Chakra).**

– Next, after 6/9 minutes, move lower palm from navel area to **Solar Plexus Chakra (Manipura Chakra).**

– Next, after 6/9 minutes, move lower palm from solar plexus area to **Heart Chakra (Anahata Chakra).**

– Next, after 6/9 minutes, move lower palm to neck area/**Throat Chakra (Vishuddha Chakra).**

– So, in 30/45 minutes, the forehead gets energy and other 5 chakras get energy for 6/9 minutes each.

Magic Healing through Mental Affirmations

Healing the physical body is not a difficult process, but to heal the body, one should have the determination to be cured. This comes only when you love yourself, believe in yourself, and possess self respect. Loving one's own self works miracles in our lives. In order to show love for oneself, Louis L Hay, a California-based psychologist and a psychiatrist of international repute, shows the whole world as to how one can heal the self, through mental affirmations i.e. "The Mental Cause for Physical Illness and The Metaphysical Way to Overcome Them" through mental affirmations and positive attitude. She is a renowned counsellor, teacher and author of several books and a healer, who has cured & healed several thousands of people all over the world. Her famous book **'Heal Your Body'** unravels the mysteries of life, and tells everyone as to how one can heal himself.

Louis Hay says that the disease can be reversed by simply reversing mental patterns. This is possible when the person is willing to do the mental work of releasing the negative emotions and forgiving. She narrates her own childhood, with the background of being raped, when she was only five years old. She developed vaginal cancer, because cancer occurs due to deep resentment. She did not agree with doctors to operate upon her cancer, as she knew that the doctors cannot remove her cancer completely, unless she clears her old pattern of resentment from her mind. She started to work with her own teacher to clear her resentment. A lot of forgiveness work was done, along with good vegetarian raw food and detoxification of the body. She completely got rid of her cancer and proved that physical ailments are due to the mental and emotional state and one can easily get rid of the disease by changing the mental pattern. Since most of us do not know the actual mental cause of the disease, we do not know where and how to begin.

The mental thought pattern that causes most of the diseases in the physical body are criticism, anger, fear, worry, frustration, jealousy, resentment and guilt. Continuous criticism can lead to arthritis. Anger causes boils, skin problems. Resentment held for a long time can ultimately lead to tumours and cancer. Guilt always seeks punishment and leads to pain. After many years of research and study, her work with her clients, she prepared a reference guide to the possible & probable mental patterns behind the disease in the body.

She gave a probable mental cause for individual diseases and a new thought pattern to completely remove the disease.

New Thought Patterns for the Diseases are as follows:

Emotional Sources of Disease

Problem	Source
Accidents	Expressions of anger, frustration, rebellion.
Anorexia/ Bulimia	Self-hate, denial of life nourishment, "not good enough."
Arms	Ability to embrace, old emotions held in joints.
Arthritis	Pattern of criticism of self and others, perfectionism.
Asthma	Smothered love, guilt complex, inferiority complex.
Back	Upper: not feeling supported emotionally, needing support. Middle: guilt. Lower: burnout, worrying about money.
Breasts	Mothering, over-mothering a person/thing/place/ experiences. Breast cancer: deep resentment attached to over-mothering.

Burns, Boils, Fevers, Itis, Sores, Swellings, Anger.

Problem	Source
Cancer	Deep resentment, distrust, self-pity, hopelessness, helplessness.
Colon	Constipation is inability to let go, lack of trust of having enough, hoarding, diarrhoea is fear of holding.
Ears	Too hard to accept what is said.
	Earaches: anger.
	Deafness: refusal to listen.
Feet	Self-understanding, moving forward.
Fingers	Index: ego, anger and fear.
	Thumb: worry.
	Middle: anger, right: a man ; left: a woman.
	Hold with other hand to release.

	Ring: unions and grief.
	Little: family and pretending.
Genitals	Femininity or masculinity issues, rejecting sexuality, "sex is dirty", "women's bodies are unclean." Bladder infections: being pissed off, holding in hurts.
	Vaginitis: romantically hurt by a partner.
	Prostate: self-worth and sexual prowess.
	Impotence: fear or spite against mate.
	Frigidity: fear, sexual guilt, self-disgust.
	PMS: denial of female cycles or female worth.
	VD: sexual guilt.
Hands	Holding on too tightly to money or relationships.
	Arthritis: self-criticism, internalizing criticism, criticizing others.
Head	Us, what we show the world, something radically wrong.
Headaches	Invalidating the self.
Heart	Heart is love and blood is joy. Heart attacks are a denial and squeezing out of love and joy.
Knees	Inflexibility, unable to bend, pride, ego, stubbornness, fear of change, self-righteousness.
Legs	Fear or reluctance of moving forward, not wanting to move. Varicose veins: standing where we hate.
Lungs	Inability to take in and give out life, denial of life. Emphysema or too much smoking: denial of life, inferiority.
Migraines	Anger and perfectionism, frustration. Masturbate to stop.
Neck	Flexibility issues.
Overweight	Needing protection, insecurity.
Pain	Guilt seeking punishment, notice where it manifests.

Sinus	Irritated by someone.
Skin	Threatened individuality, others have power over you. Thin skinned, feeling skinned alive, need self-nurturing.
Stiffness	Stiff body: stiff mind, inflexibility, fear, "only one way", resistance to change. Where manifests: where pattern is.
Stomach	Inability to digest ideas and experiences. Who or what can your stomach? Fear.
Strokes	Negative thinking, stopping of joy, forcing change of direction.
Swelling	Stagnated thinking, bottled-up tears, feeling trapped.
Throat	Fear of change, inability to speak up, anger, frustrated creativity. Laryngitis: too angry to speak; sore throat: anger; tonsillitis or thyroid: stifled creativity, deeply stifled creativity in leukemia.
Tumours	False growth, tormenting an old hurt, not allowing healing. Uterine tumours: nursing slights to femininity, misogyny.
Ulcers	Fear, not being good enough, lack of self-worth.

Reiki Treatment for Common Problems

For all treatments, except emergency cases, give treatment to full body for a minimum of 3 days continuously. After 3 days, treat as given below:

Disease		Treatment Points
Addiction	:	21 days full body treatment and then 1, 2, 3, 4, 5, 7, 8, 9, 13, 14, 19, 20, 21, 23, 24 for 3 min. each.
Asthma	:	1, 2, 3, 4, 5, 7, 8, 9 for 3 min. each, 11 for 6 min. and 13, 14 for 3 min. each.
Bad eyesight	:	1 for 3 min. 2 for 9 min. and 3, 4 for 3 min. each and 5 for 9 min.

99

Blood Pressure	:	1, 2, 4, 5 for 3 min. each, 6 for 6 min. and 7, 8, 9, 13, 14 for 3 min. each.
Burns	:	1, 2, 8 and on the spot.
Cold and cough	:	1, 2, 3, 4 for 3 min. each 6, 8, 9, 10, 11 for 6 min. each and 13 for 9 min.
Depression	:	See tension.
Diabetes	:	1, 2, 3, 4, 5, 8, 9, 10 for 3 min. each, 12 for 6-9 min. and 13, 22 for 3 min. each.
Diarrhoea	:	1, 2, 3, 4, 5, 8, 9, 10, 13, 14 for 6 min. each.
Ear pain	:	3 for 10 min.
Fever	:	1, 2 for 3 min. each and 4, 6, 8, 9, 10, 13, 14 for 6 min. each.
Fracture	:	1, 2, 8, 13 and on the spot.
Headache	:	1, 2, 3, 4, 5 for 3 min. each and 8, 9, 13 for 6 min. each.
Hearing problem	:	1, 3, 4, 7, 8, 9, 13, 14, 19, 20, 21, 23, 24 for 9 min. each.
Infertility	:	1, 2, 3, 4, 5, 7, 8, 9, 13 for 3 mins. each and 14 for 6 min.
Migraine	:	1, 2, 3, 4, 6, 8 for 3 min. each, 9, 10 for 6 min. each, and 13 for 3 min.
Obesity	:	1, 2, 3, 4, 5 for 3 min. each, 7 for 9 min., 8, 9 for 3 min. each, 13 for 6 min. and 14 for 6 min.
Paralysis	:	Continuous full body with more time on affected part.
Piles	:	1, 2, 4, 7, 8, 9 for 3 min. each, 13, 14 for 6 min. each, 19, 20, 21 for 3 min. each and 23 and 24 for 9 min. each.
Spondilytis	:	1, 2, 3, 4, 5, 6, 7, 8, 9, 13, 14 for 3 min. each and 19, 20, 21, 23, 24 for 6 min. each.
Tension	:	1, 2, 3, 4, 5 for 3 min. each, and 7, 8, 9, 13, 14 for 6 min. each.
Weakness	:	1 to 6 for 3 min. each and 8, 9, 13, 14 for 6-9 min. each.

■ ■ ■

100

5. Development of Reiki Abroad

Reiki Research Abroad

(From **Reiki News** of summer 1995, published by the Centre for Reiki Training Southfield Michigan, USA)

Scientific research in the area of laying-on hands had been conducted for some time. There are now quite a few experiments that validate the usefulness of Reiki-like healing techniques. Some of the more interesting results of these experiments demonstrate that their positive results are coming from more than just the placebo effect, while others indicate that the energy is non-physical in nature in that the benefits do not diminish regardless of the distance between sender and receiver. The following are few of the more interesting experiments.

Wendy Wetzel, a registered nurse, describes a Reiki experiment she conducted, in her paper, "Reiki Healing: A Physiologic Perspective ." In her study, 48 people made up the experimental group while 10 made up a control group. Both groups had blood samples taken at the beginning and at the end of the experiment. The experimental group received First Degree Reiki training. The control group was not involved in the Reiki training.

The blood samples were measured for haemoglobin and haematocrit values. Haemoglobin is the part of red blood cells that carry oxygen. Haematocrit is the ratio of red blood cells to total blood volume. The people in the experimental group who received Reiki training, experienced a significant change in these values with 28 per cent experiencing an increase and the remainder experiencing a decrease. The people in the control group, who did not receive Reiki training, experienced no significant change. It is thought that changes, whether an increase or decrease, are consistent with the purpose of Reiki which is to bring balance on an individual basis.

One individual experienced a 20% increase in these values. She continued to treat herself with Reiki daily and after three months, her increase had been maintained and, in fact, had continued to improve. This improvement was appropriate for her as she had been experiencing iron deficiency anaemia.

Another experiment using a Reiki like technique has also demonstrated its ability to increase haemoglobin values. A medical doctor, Otelia Bengssten, M.D., conducted an experiment with a group of 79 sick patients. Together the patients had a wide rage of diagnosed illness including pancreatitis, brain tumour, emphysema, multiple endocrine disorders, rheumatoid arthritis, and congestive heart failure. Laying-on hands treatments were given to 46 patients with 33 as controls. The treated patients showed significant increase in haemoglobin values. The effect was so pronounced that even cancer patients, who were being treated with bone marrow-suppressive agents which predictably induce decreases in haemoglobin values, showed an increase. The majority of patients also reported improvement or complete disappearance of symptoms. Both this experiment and one stated above demonstrate that healers are able to induce actual biological improvements in the patients they treat rather than simply create a feeling of well-being.

Laying-on hands healing has been validated by experiments carried out at St. Vincent's Medical Centre in New York. The experiment was carried out by Janet Quinn, Assistant Director of nursing at the University of South Carolina. The design of this experiment tends to rule out the placebo effect. Thirty heart patients were given a 20 question psychological test to determine their level of anxiety. Then they were treated by a group trained in laying-on hands healing. A control group of patients were also treated by sham healers who imitated the same positions as those who had training. Anxiety levels dropped by 17 per cent only after five minutes treatment by trained practitioners, but those who were only imitating a treatment, created no effect.

Daniel Wirth of Healing Sciences International in California conducted a tightly controlled experiment involving a Reiki-like healing technique. Forty-four male college students received identical minor wounds deliberately inflicted by a doctor in the right or left shoulder. Twenty-three then received a Reiki-like healing and the other twenty-one did not. The treatment was given in such a way that the possibility of a placebo effect was ruled out. All forty-four students extended their arms through a hole in the wall in the other room. A trained healer was present for those who received healing and administered healing from a distance without touching. From those who did not receive healing, no one was present in the room. Both the students and the doctor who administered the wounds and later also evaluated their healing rate, had been told that the experiment was about the electrical conductivity of the body. Neither knew that the experiment was about healing. Eight and sixteen days follow-up measurements of the rate of wound healing were done. After eight days, the treated groups' wounds had shrunk 93.5 per cent compared with 67.3 per cent for those not treated. After sixteen days, the figures were 99.3 and 90.9.

After debriefing, the students stated they did not know the true nature of the experiment and had felt no contact with the healer. The possibility that expectations to the students caused the healing, was ruled out.

Dr. John Zimmeman of the University of Colorado using a SQUID (Superconducting Quantum Interference Device) had discovered that magnetic fields, several hundred times stronger, are created around the hands when trained healers undertake healing work on patients. No such fields are created by 'sham' healers making the same movements indicating something special is happening with the trained healers. The frequencies of the magnetic fields surrounding the hands of the trained healers were of the alpha and that wave range similar to those seen in the brain of meditators.

Dr. Barmard Grade of McFill University in Montreal used barley seeds to test the effect of psychic healing energies on plants. The seeds were planted in pots and watered with a saline solution which is known to retard their sprouting and growth. With elaborate doubleblind conditions set up, one group of seeds were watered with saline held by the healer in sealed container for fifteen minutes. The other seeds were watered with untreated saline. The person watering the plants did not know which group was getting the treated saline and which was getting the untreated saline. The plants watered with healer treated saline solution grew faster and were healthier producing 25% more weight and having a higher chlorophyll content. These experiments have been replicated in Dr. Grad's lab and in other laboratories as well.

Dr. Grad carried out similar experiments involving tap water and plants. Sealed containers of water were given to a psychic healer to hold and others were given to a severely depressed patient to hold. The plants watered with the healer held water had an increased growth rate & those watered with the water, held by the severely depressed patient, had a decrease in growth rate compared to controls.

These experiments involving plants, in addition to confirming the non-placebo nature of psychic healing, scientifically confirm the ancient metaphysical understanding that healing energies can be stored in water for future use.

In another experiment involving psychic healer Olga Worrall, Dr. Robert Miller used an electromechanical transducer to measure the microscopic growth rate of rye grass. The device used has an accuracy of one thousandth of an inch per hour. Dr. Miller set up the experiment in his laboratory and then left, locking the door behind him to eliminate any unnecessary disturbance. Olga was located over 600 miles away.

When Dr. Miller returned to the laboratory the next day, the test equipment had recorded normal continuous growth of 6.25 thousandths of an inch per hour up to 9 PM. At that time, the record began to deviate upward and had risen to 52.5 thousandths of an inch per hour which was an increase of 840 per cent! This increased growth rate remained till morning when it decreased but never to its original level.

The Soindrift group has done extensive research involving prayer on plants. Their results indicate that prayed-for-plants always grow faster and are healthier than non-prayed-for-plants even though the conditions are equal for both groups of plants and those doing the praying are miles away. These results were consistent regardless of the distance involved and occurred over and over. One of the interesting results of their research work is that they were best when the prayer was non-directional, that is when the prayer was simply for the plants' general well-being rather than for a specific result, such as a certain growth rate or overall height.

More experiments are being done and scientific theories are being developed to describe Reiki and Reiki like healing techniques. As we continue into the new millennium, increasing interest along with more sensitive equipment will allow science to more completely understand, validate, and accept the reality of Reiki. As this happens, we will see increasing use of Reiki and other laying-on hands healing coming into common use by individuals for themselves and family along with its use in hospitals and doctor's offices. With a deeper understanding about the nature of health and the unity of all life, this rediscovered age old wisdom will reduce suffering and make our Earth a more worthwhile place to live in. With this in mind, let us be encouraged to continue in the spirit of Reiki to help others and to heal the planet.

■ ■ ■

Bibliography

1. Jarell, d-Reiki Plus Institute, Hibernia West, Rt 3 Box 313 Celina, TN 38551. *Reiki Manual – Heal Yourself* by Riedel, D. Book and Manuals.

2. *The Reiki Handbook* by Arnold L & Nevius, S.-PSL Press, Para Science International, 1025 Miller Lane, Harrisburg, PA 171102899.

3. *Reiki – Universal Life Force Energy* by Baginsky, B. & Sharamon, S.-Life Rythem, P.O. Box 806, Mendocino, CA95460.

4. *Reiki – Howayo Takata's Story* by Haberly. M Archedigm.

5. *Empowerment Through Reiki* by Horan, Paula-Lotus Light Publications, P. O. Box 2, Wilmot, WI53192.

6. *Virginia Samdahl-Reiki Master* by Lugenbeel, B Gunwald and Radcliff Publishers, Norfolk, VA.

7. *The Reiki Factor* by Ray Barbara, Expositions Press Inc., Smithtown, New York, USA.

8. *The Reiki Touch* by Stewart J. C.-Reiki Touch Inc., Houston, Texas, USA.

9. *The Official Reiki Handbook* by Ray B. and Carrington, YAIRA, P. O. Box 40570, St. Petersburg, Florida 33743-0570, USA.

10. *The Reiki Alliance,* P.O. Box 41. Cataldo, Idaho 83810-1041, USA.

11. *Reiki – The Healing Touch* by Rand William, Vision Publications, 29209, Northwestern Hwy., 522 South Field, ML48034, USA.

12. *Light Emerging – The Journey of Personal Healing* by Barbara Ann Brennan.

13. *Hands of Light – A Guide to Healing through the Human Energy Field* by Barbara Ann Brennan.

14. *Essential Reiki – A Complete Guide to an Ancient Healing Art* by Diane Stein.

15. *Chakras – Energy Centres of Transformation* by Harish Johari.

■■■

Glossary

Ahankar : (Sanskrit): False ego, illusory identification of one's position or essential self.

Annamaya Kosha : (Ayurveda): The sheath covering the essential spiritual self made of foodstuffs. (anna: foodgrains.)

Ascension : To initiate growth, also known as "raising or awakening the Kundalini".

Atma : (Sanskrit): "The Self", the soul: The essential, pure non-material, and unchanging element in all living beings, the symptom of which is consciousness.

Attitude of Gratitude : (a) The invocation made at the beginning and end of each Reiki healing; (b) The state of being in an attitude of thankfulness for everything in one's life.

Attunement : The process of connecting individuals to the Reiki energies through a confidential and mystic process, empowering them to heal their bodies and their lives. Also known as diksha or spiritual initiation.

Aura : The human energy field, the pranamaya kosha as identified by Ayurveda. It can also be termed as electromagnetic field around the physical body.

Chakra : (Sanskrit): Wheel, spinning vortex of energy in the human energy field (aura) that works as energy accumulator and pump. The major chakras correspond to the endocrine system of the physical body and nerve plexuses (ganglia). Also known as the "consciousness" or "perception plexuses". (See also "Nadi").

Channel	:	A person who is initiated as a channel for making available the Reiki healing energy.

Chemicalisation : An unpleasant yet favourable process: the release of biochemical waste products (toxins) from the physical body's disease sites in response to healing which may result in some temporary resurgence of old symptoms or conditions.

Clairvoyant : A person having "clear vision", who can see the human energy field (aura). Rare clairvoyants can see past and future events in depth with clarity. The Vedic term for such persons is *trikal-darshi*: one who can see all three areas of time: past, present, future, in the material as well as spiritual worlds where time is a single continuum. Many Reiki channels start developing this and other hidden mystic talents soon after their Reiki connection.

Cleansing : Synonymous with chemicalisation, but generally covers a wider range of activities including release of toxins physically, emotionally and in one's life situations. A change or shift taking place here in stages for the ultimate benefit of the healee.

Cosmic Energy : It is the combination of all the five basic elements i.e. EARTH, AIR, WATER, FIRE and ETHER. It is also known as Pancha-Maha-Bhuta or Pancha Tattva.

Diksha : (Sanskrit): Formal initiation and empowerment procedure for linking our bodily matter with the Divine.

Empowerment	:	Active authorization in the context of Reiki healing, the receipt, establishment and activation of the Reiki healing energy in an individual.
False Ego	:	The illusory identification of self with the perishable expansion of matter, the three material modes of nature: mode of goodness (sattvic-guna), mode of passion (rajo-guna), mode of ignorance (tamo-guna); also known as sattva, rajas, ta:nas: Goodness, Passion and Ignorance.
Grandmaster	:	A highly developed Master of Reiki, who is spiritually enlightened enough, so as to be able to reveal authentic hidden knowledge of Reiki and the spiritual light according to time, place and circumstance, by direct perception of the Truth. A Grandmaster is also a "Master of Masters" and able to heal and enlighten even advance spiritualists such as genuine Reiki Masters. A Grandmaster's appearance is relatively rare.
Healee	:	The person, place, or situation receiving the healing whether in the present, past or future.
Healer	:	The individual through whom the healing is being channelled. For convenience, a Reiki channel may refer to himself as a "healer", but he knows that the healing results come from elsewhere and that he is only a channel to make available the healing energy.
Human Energy Field	:	See "Aura"
Initiation	:	Synonymous with attunement and diksha.
Karma	:	(Sanskrit): "Activity, work" which brings a certain resuit or reaction. Karma and vikarma refer to desirable and undesirable

110

(good-bad) result-generating activity. A karma refers to that activity which does not generate "good-bad" results but actually liberates one from the karma syndrome.

This is a pure healing spiritual activity only, currently best available through Reiki as evidenced through the results that are available for anyone who receives a proper authorized Reiki connection and practises self-healing.

Kosh : "Sheath" or covering, housing the essential pure, non-material, undamageable and unchanging element (the Soul), the symptom of which is consciousness.

Kundalini : The body's vital energy.

Kundalini Syndrome : The untimely or improper rising of the kundalini energy resulting in difficult undiagnosed and undiagnosable disease and illness.

Lotus Sutras : Sacred Buddhist scriptures that gave the clue to Dr. Mikao Usui for his Reiki enlightenment.

Nadi : Nerve, vein/blood vessel; mainly referring to the subtle energy body (aura) through which pranic energy flows.

Negativities : Negative energies and emotions such as Anger, Jealousy, Hatred, Envy, Fear, Worry, Intolerance, Anxiety.

Pancha Kosha : Body consists of five Koshas or Sheaths or layers, namely:

Annamaya Kosha	:	**Physical Body**
Pranamaya Kosha	:	**Mental Body**
Manomaya Kosha	:	**Emotional Body**
Vignanamaya Kosha	:	**Intellectual Body**
Anandamaya Kosha	:	**Spiritual Body**

111

Prana	:	Life sustaining subtle energy of the nature of electricity and lightning which flows in the aura body of all living beings, available from air, sun, water, earth, food.
Pranamaya Kosha	:	The sheath made from pranic energy which provides a vehicle for the pure spiritual self, the atma or soul.
Pranic Healing	:	An energy healing modality utilizing pranic energy from the air which works directly on the pranamaya kosha of the individual. Pranic healing works across space but not time, does not require any special empowerment (diksha), but requires much dedicated practice and personal spiritual elevation. It takes about three to seven years of practice to become a competent pranic healer, as compared to three months for a Reiki healer.
Reiki	:	**Universal life force energy.**
Reiki Master	:	Initiating Master and Teacher of Reiki.
Reincarnation	:	The reappearance or rebirth of individual consciousness in different life-forms according to individual desire and activities (karma).
Santana Dharma	:	(Sanskrit): "The eternal occupational duty and categorical position of mankind". The highest connection in this system is stated to be that of **unconditional love,** in other words, of **Reiki.**
Shuddh Sattva	:	The mode or state of pure spiritual quality, such as available with Reiki.
Soul	:	The elemental, vital animating life principle, pure spiritual particle of individual consciousness present in all living beings.

■■■